Swimming for the Ark

ALSO BY JOAN MURRAY

The Same Water

Looking for the Parade

Queen of the Mist

Dancing on the Edge

Poems to Live By in Uncertain Times (editor)

Poems to Live By in Troubling Times (editor)

The Pushcart Book of Poetry: the Best Poems from 30 Years of the Pushcart Prize (editor)

Swimming for the Ark

New & Selected Poems
1990 – 2015

Joan Murray

Distinguished Poets Series

WHITE PINE PRESS / BUFFALO, NEW YORK

White Pine Press
P.O. Box 236, Buffalo, New York 14201
www.whitepine.org

Grateful acknowledgment is made to the publishers of the books and journals in which these poems, or their earlier versions, originally appeared:
Poems from *Dancing on the Edge* by Joan Murray, copyright © 2002 by Joan Murray. Used by permission of Beacon Press.

"20th Century Creativity," "Autumn in Eden," "The Black Dog," "Breath," "The Good 'Bad Kids'," "Her Head," "Looking for the Parade," "Peterborough Pet Store," "Play by Play," "Possession," "Sonny's Hands," "Taking the Count," "What to Do with an Inchworm" from *Looking for the Parade* by Joan Murray. Copyright © 1999 by Joan Murray. Used by permission of W. W. Norton & Company, Inc.

Additional acknowledgments appear on page 202, which constitutes an extension of this copyright page.

Publication of this book was made possible, in part, by grants from Amazon.com; the National Endowment for the Arts, which believes that a great nation deserves great art; and with public funds from the New York State Council on the Arts, a State Agency.

Cover art: *Swimmer* by James T. McClellan. Used by permission of the CAPE ANN MUSEUM, Gloucester, MA, photo by Robinson McClellan.

Author photo by David Lee.

First Edition

ISBN: 978-1-935210-63-4

Printed and bound in the United States of America.

Library of Congress Control Number: 2014930819

CONTENTS

NEW POEMS

THE SAME WATER (1990)

QUEEN OF THE MIST (1999)

LOOKING FOR THE PARADE (1999)

DANCING ON THE EDGE (2002)

äntligen för min mor

Vera Björk Schwetje

NEW POEMS

CONTENDER

I could have been that woman
in the sequined dress, standing up at the Steinway,
or the man in the collarless linen suit,
pleased by the prices his gallery set,
or that woman from Kenya in crimson silks,
the tape breaking across my chest,
or the chestnut horse whipped to a froth
with roses around my neck.
But I balked, I balked, I gave up too soon
at the bench where my mother taught me how.
Never try to tell me anything, just let me run.

And all my art professors with their
follow-me agendas, never once saying
"be" instead of "do." I was no one's mirror, no one's
pacer, no one's ingénue. I ran, and I could run
but I couldn't throw. The ball dropped here
where anyone could be. If only God
hadn't twitched that night when he breathed a
speck of life into the air while my parents,
still shy with each other, lay together,
I could have been that bird with the yellow breast,
or I l have ben a flower, any flower.

FAMILY DOLLAR

The New Choice Pregnancy Testing Kits
are hung along the ramp-up to the register.
The woman ahead of me would pass hers
with flying colors. She's huge and sighing,
the kids in her cart keep eying my candy.
I recognize the cashier—she's the girl
who used to work at the Video Cave that closed.
We saw her one time after that—at the go-kart place—
she told us she'd moved away, she had won
some kind of scholarship, and was going to
start college in Syracuse. We watched
her boyfriend race her around the track,
he made her howl with such abandon
when he rammed her.

The house just east of the go-kart place
caved in a month ago. It had been peeling
and boarded up for years. When I'd drive by,
I used to say, *I bet there's something*
good in there. Then one night last July,
I watched three guys come out, they were
carrying the stairs. But who do you call
if you see a thing like that, where do you start—
do you just say, *Send a cruiser right away,*
I just saw someone taking a flight of stairs?
I wonder if she'll remember me—I remember
she was smart. The lines here take a lifetime,
but it's easy to fill your cart. When everything
is next to nothing.

WHAT WAS EXPECTED

It wasn't his ugliness that startled me. It was mostly
that he hadn't been expected, and when I flipped on the porch light,
he was eating from the cats' bowl, and when I tapped
the frost-edged glass, he looked up, the way the cats do,
and then he waited through that moment
of not knowing what was next—
as if I were Peter at the Gate, and it could go either way.
I tried to squeeze his opossum shape, his oversized
head and pointed snout, his dull black eyes and wormy tail
into the tidy image of a cat that I'd brought to the door with me.

But even though we gave it our best,
we realized, almost right away, that it was impossible,
and we had to pool our efforts and do what was
expected: I had to pull the door open—even though
the threat it made at that point was less than a child's bluff—
and once it had been done, he had to back away from the bowl,
giving up the incomprehensible gift he'd just come upon,
and slink down the steps—not quickly, mind you,
because he guessed, dumb beggar, I wouldn't pursue him,
only leave him to his hunger and the dicey scraps of winter
as the stars did in December when he came.

But it wasn't as if I could lift the kitchen window and throw
him a nickel or a dime and watch him go away happy—
the way we did back in the City,
when the *beggars*—that's what my mother
called them—would come in winter
to sing in the backyards below our apartment windows
with their clear bright faces and beautiful voices
and the mystery of the coins ringing down from above,
rolling and skipping, and them bending and scraping

and tipping their hats and going away,
even though we weren't rich either.

No, he was more like the ones we'd come upon
in the places where we were forbidden to go,
the ones our mothers called *bums*—the crazy wild-eyed
grizzled ones, lying on their slit cardboard boxes
under the bridge ramps even in winter,
or raving along the tracks with their hands down their pants
because of the lice, or pissing in an alley as we ran through
and slowly turning midstream to call after us—
Have you got a nickel or a dime?—the ugly
ones, the ones who had no songs, the ones
with nothing to give us.

THE COPIER

The copier's still working despite the coat of dust.
There still are marriages to be recorded. And divorces,
of course. And deeds to be transferred—
think of all those acres to be scooped up on the square
where there used to be a market with flutes and setars,
and a Baghdad bride in a wide,
white, Western gown, and a small boy guiding a wheelchair
with his grandmother through the stalls.
There were pyramids of fruit. And chicken on spits.
Souvlaki. Black coffee. And a tiled
pool with fish, where a girl in pigtails
called out to passersby, and a bus sped by with
two men hanging from its sides, and everyone
smiling for the camera, everyone waving
and making their peace signs just as we do.

But all that was years ago—
before we gave them their freedom
and made their place a ruin. Just rubble and dust,
even so, it's somebody's bargain—even though
those other things—those buses and flutes,
setars and fruit, and everyone smiling and
making their peace signs and railing
against their leader just as we do—have been
moved to other scenes. And there's only this one left now:
just the copier and his son, it's a black and white
one—I'll scan it if you like, and in no time
you'll have them in their dusty room. The copier
with his ink pot. And his young son
watching every stroke, watching as the deeds
are recorded, keeping track of
what's been done, and who will pay for it.

THE GYPSY CHILD

Was it only last winter when I opened the cabinet
and found that half-eaten bag of confectioners' sugar
and the confetti of droppings that moved me
like a child's finger-painting that says "YOU"?
It forced me to reconsider the universal "truth"
that a mouse is a creature whose big ecstasy
is coming across a seed or two.
No, that's only the hunter-gatherers.
Give a mouse the run of your house
and it will beat a path to your bag of sugar
and gorge itself with a happiness that
could move you to tears, which is what
I gave it, right there—with my fingers
in the mess it had left me.

But today, coming across the pound cake on the counter,
with a quarter of it missing, and an orgy of droppings
on the birthday napkins on the Lazy Susan,
I damned it and promised it its death.
And now I'm left with what I've lost—
the simple capacity to be stirred by simple things
like *unabashed greed* and *discriminating appetite,*
which led it, human-like, to bypass
the bowl of apples and the sacks of navy beans.
But the difference isn't between
mere sugar and *consummate* cake—
I didn't make the cake myself, I've got no personal
stake in the seconds of someone's life
that got nibbled off with it.

This has more to do with the way you're
not designed to moisten up

at the end of a movie you've already seen—
Maybe sympathy comes best
when it's got some element of surprise to it—
like when you stop on 14th Street and reach
for your wallet the first time the Gypsy child
grabs your arm and tells you she's hungry.
But the next time, though she's probably
just as hungry, which may be
considerably or not at all,
you push her hand away.
And the next time, you push her harder
and call her an ugly name.

THE IVORY BILLED ONE

It's not because it's beautiful—
actually it's a lot like the pileated one—
ugly, even scary to some, a small pterodactyl.
It's partly because of how long
it's been missing, and how we thought
we killed it, and even if we didn't, there'd be a lot
less answering to do for everything else,
if we could bring it back.

One gets spotted every six or seven years
by someone who's mistaken or insane or
whose camera is deficient or who
goes insane when he's called a liar.
And partly because we miss things
when they're gone and don't come back,
like Armenia and Jesus and the Old World Jews
and Diana on her long legs in the land mines.

But every now and then, one shows up
in the woods behind some parking lot—
but before you can grab
your cell phone to catch it on the wing,
it's already missing and you're
feeling bereft and starting to go insane
as you step into the woods, wondering
what's next and if they'll miss you.

LOOKING AT THE BIRDS

I

My father had two Audubon books
with more birds than you could see in a lifetime.
Each one busy and purposeful, taking its
birdness seriously. They were also pretty—
like the crooked-necked one with a wild hairdo
—though I couldn't read their names.
I was three or four, and they were only
pictures in the books—except for the owls,
one brown, one white, who stared at me
while the other birds looked away
—*Is* that *why I stared back at them ?*
Or was it the mouse or the rabbit—
prostrate on the earth or snow. The frank,
unhurried mess of blood. A single talon,
sufficient as a word. A game that was
played for keeps. Something shameful.
I knew. Instinctively. I let no one
see me see. The huge eyes saying, *You.*
What are you staring at? Do you like it?
As if all vision is complicity.
As if they knew I would look again.

II

In the parallel tracks of my bedspread,
I ran two rows of pennies—Lincolns racing Lincolns
from my pillow to the hideout by my feet.
A common sort of game. Maybe you played it too
when you were five. Maybe *someone* played with you.
When I looked across the street, I could see a row of stores:
Ryan's Deli which sold *head cheese* (which was meat),
OK Cleaners with a calendar I wasn't supposed to see,
a Chinese laundry run by a German refugee,
and a nursery where my mother threatened
to send me every day. I'd watch the girls my age
line up beside their cots and go to sleep when they
were told. And behind them, Noonan Towers—
a building tall enough to have an elevator—
between whose towers at night I sometimes saw the stars
—and, one day, looking up, I watched two curtains part
on a man in a bathrobe in a window—
It was open—did he know?—did he see me?
When my mother came, I told her I was
looking at the birds. She said I'd seen enough that day.
Yet for eight years he was there to see me off to school:
Each morning when my best friend came
and called me from the street, he'd
appear before I made it down the stairs.
When I was little, I sometimes thought he flew.

III

When I turned fourteen, I took the D train north—
against the crowds. Most days the car was empty,
though every week or so, there'd be a man—
whispering, silent, or raving—staring straight at me
or at the ceiling. And whether he was white or black or gray,
walking up and down, or blocking the way to
another car, or sitting across from me, or leaning against a pole—
It was open—it was out—it was waving.
I'd drop my head in Dickens, yet he kept me in his game
—and played his hand to win. He got off. Before I did.
Then I'd walk the ten blocks from the station
to a school with tidy, proper girls, who came
from under canopies with matching chests and
other sets of reference and different points of view,
which allowed them to regard me with indifference.
One day in Mrs. Koeffler's class, we had to
name the stars: she asked me who Orion was,
she wouldn't let me go. *O'Ryan, was an Irish God,*
I tried. I had to rig a smile till their laughter died.
All that year, I watched those girls line up for lunch—
in their polished shoes and hand-pressed pleats
that were never crushed on trains, I'd watch them
heap their trays with piles of sweets and fruit, I'd watch
the way they'd grip their bananas, their mouths
open wide, thinking they knew everything.

MAX AND ROSE

I didn't know then
how couples flow into the space around each other—
how Max's sweet exuberance
was only made possible by Rose's bitter chill.
Who knew what that whole generation
of refugees had gone through?
I knew nothing about them—
only that Max had been to Alaska,
had prospected for gold. Said words like
Klondike, Ketchikan, Kodiak. Stirred our imaginations
like the Yukon claim deeds in our cereal box.
It was the South Bronx. I was seven. He called me
Joan of Arc. My brother, *Charles de Galle.* For a dime,
we'd get a Sunday scoop of ice cream,
and a chance for some tall tale.
But Rose with her long sighs roused only
one question: *Why* did he marry her?
If we'd see her heading to the counter,
we knew already all was lost. Silent as frost,
she'd slosh the metal scoop through the trough
of cloudy water, then dig, dig, dig—
like a prisoner hacking at a rock
that was ten-times-ten impossible—
and we were the ones who were forcing her.
If it were Max, the cone would sail forward
in his hand. Solid. Immense. Like the dense
block of an igloo. But Rose
with her sighs slipped in pockets
of air. Gaps. Evasions.
Places to hide.

THE WITCH'S DAUGHTER

The witch, we knew. Because she lived below
the cliff we scrambled over. And she yelled
ten times worse than anybody's mother. So the witch
was the one we took everyone to see. First, we'd
creep along the cliff edge soundlessly, then let out
a scream of laughter. Oh how the witch
detested laughter. To her it was a dog ripping out
her throat, or a knife doodling in her gut, or the fat
Monsignor sitting down and squeezing all her air out.

But the witch's daughter never came out. The witch's
daughter made herself invisible with a spell.
Yet now and then, we'd see the pair of them,
walking together, step by step, trying hard to look normal,
step by step, putting one foot down and then the other,
like everyone else on Ogden Avenue, till we couldn't
stand it a second longer, and someone had to shout,
Look out, it's the witch and the witch's daughter!
And we'd dive between two cars and hide for our lives.

But sometimes in the hallway of the school
we'd see the witch's daughter without her mother,
looking like any other kid, looking almost like us
in her brilliant disguise of an ugly blue uniform
and even having a kid's name like the rest of us,
till someone had to shout, *Look out, it's the witch's daughter!*
And then she would run. All the way home to her mother.
Where she could be as evil as a mountain. And as cold
as the dark. And as invisible as a star.

JUST TASTE THEM

My mother spread them on the metal kitchen table:
Edam, Gouda, Havarti, Chevre,
Jarlsberg, Camembert, Stilton.
I don't remember why there were seven,
but that night I wondered, if you did it at all,
if there had to be seven
like the sacraments.

What I liked best were their names: seven whole
new things to put on your tongue, as well as smell
and especially taste them, and even chew them,
unlike Communion, and my mother
cutting them into delicate bits, not
slices or hunks, like when my father
wanted something late at night—

no, just delicate bits like rhinestones or quarters,
and my mother lifting them to me
on a toothpick or a cracker, and the two of us saying
their names before we tasted them, like we were
earning the taste by saying it, and not the usual
saltines either, not like when my father
wanted something fast.

She never called it a *tasting,* maybe she knew
that was its name, maybe from some magazine
she'd picked up at the check-out, one of those ones
that shows the consolations of food and flowers,
but we didn't live in a place where
people had *tastings,* so all we could do
was just taste them.

I kept picturing when my father would come home later
from his job at Madison Square Garden
and would kneel to see what was in the fridge
and would come upon those odd-named things
and wonder what they were doing there—
as if they'd come from somewhere very far away—
the food of some strangers
or maybe their gods.

THE GARDENER'S WIFE

That summer in the mound of sand
someone left beside the cesspool lid,
my father managed to grow a watermelon—
it's not what you're picturing—maybe not even edible,
the size of a softball, but, hell, it was a watermelon,
and all year round, the man worked two jobs in the City,
and only came out on summer weekends, but he knelt down
and planted it. From a seed. With a kid's shovel.
And every weekend he tended it by hand,
he put up twigs and twine, he weeded, watered,
the way God must have done before he brought in
the gardener and the gardener's wife
and everything went wrong.

My father said he "got a kick out of it"—
he liked to say that about lots of things—
not just watermelons, cats and dogs, his children even.
My mother watched him, watched the way
he knew how to be happy over nothing,
and on Mondays when he got the train back to the City,
she would take her tools from the old outhouse that we now
had to call "the shed"—her trimmers and pruners,
her clippers and scythe—and the pole with the saw-toothed hook
that could reach up and take down anything.
But she didn't need them for that watermelon,
I mean, someone could just pick it up
and chuck it into the bushes like a ball.

SWIMMING FOR THE ARK

Because the hurricane was coming, and because
he wasn't there, and because his boat was moored
off the public beach, roped to an empty
Clorox jug with cinder blocks beneath,
my father told my mother to go and save it.

He had spoken to her, as he did every Wednesday,
when we went by flashlight to the phone booth by
the juke box in the Sweet Shop
and pushed our way through the crush of
teenagers who rippled there in the dim light with

their tall, glinting bodies, their cigarettes
and music. And my mother closed herself
into the phone booth like the Virgin ascending to heaven,
and I was left outside in the drowning noise,
where my ten-year-old eyes

could glance into the phone booth and see
her sweating under the gaze of the high-wattage bulb
while all the pale flimsy things that worshipped the light
flitted around her, and she lifted her soaked arms
and held the receiver to her ear like an oracular

shell and dropped in her coins—but it was too loud
out where I was to hear them chime, and too loud
to hear his voice—though I could *see her hearing it*—
and when the door parted and the light went out,
she said we must save his boat.

It wasn't much of a boat—not much more than a dinghy—
and when we saw it in the morning it was already struggling:

thrashing at the end of its lean exhausted rope, jerking
its whiplashed bow above the pounding of the waves that
were trying to drag it in behind them.

It wasn't too far out—just beyond the rotting pilings
at the end of the dead-end road where we swam
for pleasure. My mother said we'd swim out together—
we'd gone farther hundreds of times. But the tide
was higher than it had been that whole summer—

it was halfway up the beach, and when we reached
the boat, my quavering feet couldn't touch the bottom.
She signaled me to hold it while she untied it, then
one on each side, we began to turn it so we could guide it in
—but the waves tossed me aside like a sack of kittens.

And I saw her float away—she went floating
away, hanging onto his boat—hanging onto it like she was
saving it, but it was carrying her to shore, and I was
trying to keep up, throwing myself on the waves like I was
swimming for the Ark, and I kept falling behind her.

She never turned to look for me. Maybe she
thought I was hanging onto the far side of the gunnel. Maybe
she was calling out to me. But it was too loud there
to hear her. I saw the distance between us growing—
the wind was driving us both to shore, but she had

his boat and the weight of his command and she was
going to land while *I* was still halfway out. I kept throwing
myself forward, trying to feel the bottom, and when at last

I could, I stood with my heart in my throat and saw
her let go—just before the boat slammed sideways into shore—

it rocked and swerved there and nearly struck her,
but like a mother miraculously possessed so she can
lift a runaway truck that's about to strike her child,
she grabbed the rope, jerked its bow up from the surf,
and, in one lumbering birth, dragged the whole thing out.

That's when she turned and looked for me—
and spotted me in the water, with the waves up to
my shoulders—breaking against my neck, my face,
I waved to her like a shipwrecked sailor who's
gone crazy clinging to a spar—I called to her

and saw her calling back. But it was too loud out where I
was to hear what she was saying. I imagined she was
calling my name—not knowing where I
was and being afraid for me. I imagined she could see
how exhausted I was, how glad I was to

see her calling. But then I saw the look on her face,
and I knew she was yelling—yelling at me
to stop my playing. Yelling at me to *get in right away*
and help her drag his boat to the top of the beach
so she could go and call him and tell him what she'd done.

DOORWAY

Of course we said we'd help you—
the cops were after you, you said, and we were *rebel girls,*
weren't we? the four of us fifteen, the same age
you said you were, when we crammed together
in the doorway of a gated store,
the windows full of knives, vibrators,
transistor radios.
I was the only one who understood:
Lemony blond, sweet-voiced for a boy,
you hid behind our Tangee lipstick, our teased-up
hair-dos, the wispy-angora sweaters I can see
in the photo-booth photos I still have here.

I was flattered that you liked my *pixie boots,*
my *avant garde* ring (you didn't mention
how it turned my finger green), I bought it on a street
another night I lied and took a subway to Manhattan.
It was the Village that time—someday I'd be
a painter and live there, but first I had to grow up.
We'd come to 42nd Street to pick up sailors—
though we innocents compared to you—
and when the cop spotted you in our circle
(it was the bright peroxide hair), you ran, he didn't follow,
but cornered us instead: *I've got a daughter your age,*
get back to the Bronx, he said.

He made sure we headed to the subway. Made sure
we started down the steps—where we stopped,
counted slowly to a hundred—
came up and raced around the block. What luck
to come face to face with *four* sailors in dress blues:
Some nights you get lucky, other nights you don't.

We paired up as we walked. Past windows full of negligees
and Billy clubs. Statues of Liberty and handcuffs.
We spotted you across the street,
you were leaning in a doorway, talking to a man.
You noticed us too but didn't wave back,
I hope he was good to you.

The sailors weren't what we'd been expecting—
they took us to the USO, eight free tickets
to a Broadway show, it was my first:
Great Day in the Morning with Colleen Dewhurst—
I was surprised that no one took their clothes off.
Later in their hotel room, my sailor fingered
his guitar while everybody talked, he was the shy one,
he wouldn't neck—but none of them went too far.
He showed me a wallet photo of his girl:
prom dress, blond, a little overweight,
they lived on farms in some Midwest state,
I made up a lie and got out of there.

On my way back to the subway, I looked for you
in all the doorways. But there was only
my own reflection. The seasick homesick lights.
The hooting of the revelers. The dancers
through the windows of the Metropole. The darkened
limos pulling away. A priest on the prowl,
looking for someone to save.
At the entrance to the subway, a woman rose up
and grabbed me, her long hair matted, streaked with grey,
her stained coat open, she was pregnant, close to due,
she stank of booze, asked only for a dollar.
I pushed by. I didn't look back.

But it's bright there still—all the blinking, reeling lights,
all the jittery hopeful throngs, the cops with their batons,
the limos pulling away—I wandered into Barbie's Kingdom once,
it isn't a place for you. No, it's nothing like that night
when we huddled together in a doorway—
back when your body was a crime, and someone
drove you from their lives in some other state or borough.
Where else did they think you'd go? How else
would you survive?—And for how long?
Still, every year when the ball drops at Times Square,
where our years end and begin again,
I take a sip for you, old runaway friend.

THE WELL

Mid-August near the Cliffs of Mohr, I thought of Katie
coming back from Ireland before our third year of high school,
telling me how she'd brought her bathing suit, and no one
had ever seen one, except in the movies. And underfoot,
the stones. Not sand, she said, not like we have here. Only
stones. And the whole Atlantic Ocean, and the sun
not really there, and the fog turning everywhere
green except down there where it was stones
and hard to walk on, and her shoes weren't
right and the cliffs like they'd been ripped off
the face of the moon, and the great forever out there and
where on earth would you end up if it took you?

A lifetime later walking there, I could picture her at sixteen,
turning the elbow of the road out of Doolin through
the fog and rough-going—and the stones. Maybe not the
same exact ones, but the same sort of dragged around,
pummeled-down things and the waves that some poet
might have called furious or deranged, but they were only
what they'd always been. She was dead by then.
I knew when I saw the envelope. Her husband's
name. Not hers. "She took her own life," he said.
And I pictured her young again, pale from somewhere
where there never was sun, and those dark eyebrows
that she once asked with such embarrassment, should she
tweeze?—all that shame to admit the body. And hard to believe
a daughter would come later. Slow like her laughter
that used to come up from somewhere deep, as if it had to be
dislodged from beneath something heavy like God.

The guidebook mentioned a holy well, a short walk
down the numbered road. But it seemed miles before

I found it. A *Bridget's Well*, the book said, but there was
no sign for it, not like Fatima or Lourdes. No tourists or
flashbulbs. Just a small place underground. An ante-room
opening onto another anteroom. And then what?
Just a slow pulse of water into a trough, and the cave mouth
admitting a dim swath of light, enough to see the crude
wet walls and the few disconnected pipes overhead—
wooden canes dangling off them, and beads wound around,
all embrangled together, and bleached scraps of letters,
photos curling the way they do when it's damp and thirty
years later—children mostly—and pockmarked statues
showing off their embarrassing hearts and wincing decay.

But I'm still not getting it right for you—the way the whole
thing was *one* thing: a heap of beseechings and dry-mouthed
desperation—all the brown flowers and yellowed handkerchiefs,
a child's pale braid in two tarnished barrettes, an American
dime sixty-seven years old—the slough of everyone
lowering themselves into the earth, stooping to the
water with their armloads of sorrows, not questioning
what they'd been given, only asking for something else,
and the true god Time dozing naked in the corner
where the water kept trickling, and all three Bridgets
beside him: the one who was a goddess before she
became a saint, the saint one, and the one with the
missing eye when they all were carved in stone.

One summer in Pennsylvania, my eighty-year-old neighbor,
loaned me a brittle tourist book with a photo of Cold Air Cave:
three women in white Victorian dresses and parasols to
shield them from the sun. That was before women
went to the shore, before women wore bathing suits.

They were standing in front of the cave mouth, not far
from the Water Gap, and they didn't know what to do with
their mouths because the cold damp air of the earth was on them
like the Oracle at Delphi, and it only cost a dime.
It was difficult to find at first, up on the cliff side with the
numbered highway down below and the cars whooshing by,
a few annoyed and honking because I'd left mine
on the shoulder, some slowing down to ask if I was
all right: a woman climbing up a cliff alone.
I didn't find it by sight, there was no sign either,
I went blindly till I passed a hole and felt the shock
of cold air rushing out as it's always done. "She took
her own life," her husband said. But it was hers to take or give,
and she took it out beyond the troubling stones.

WHITE BRIDGE ROAD

Awakened by the noise of morning geese,
I reach to wake my husband. The spot's
still warm. But he's gone—probably halfway
down the hill to Shaker Museum Road
where no Shakers ever lived (it's so steep it makes
his shins ache when he uses them as brakes).

Soon he'll turn onto White Bridge Road,
past the house of the woman who asked him
why he walks. "For health," he said unthinkingly.
Now she's fixed on the notion that he's ill,
and asks each morning, with an earnestness
that comes across like death, how he's feeling.

I sleep on my side with my knees up when he's here,
now a cat's curled underneath. It might be the one
I like. Or the one I don't. They warm me equally.
The doctor says there's *arthritis* in one knee—
I never told about the pain that sometimes comes there.
I never thought it had to stay. Until it got its name.

I know he sits here in the dark until he's ready for his walk
—sometimes I wake and smell the smoke.
Or hear his lips draw back in a slow sip from the cup,
he doesn't like me there. Yet he still bends down to
leave a kiss before he takes the stairs. He thinks that I'm
asleep. Since I lie here like the road. Sometimes I am.

LIFELINE

A painted turtle in the middle of the road. Plodding its way
to the Cummings' house where Max was barking
bare-teethed through the screen. And since it was mid-September,
the time for it to burrow under for the winter (under the
pond across the street, I mean), I made my
decision to be its *personal savior.* I hadn't noticed
one all summer, but I was gone for half of August
and had house guests in July. I felt a seventh-day
sort of pride as I picked it up. And matched it
to my palm. And traced its lifeline (which was at least
as long as mine) and carried it back across the road,
squeezing between the earth-machines
that the road crew left behind
when they went to lunch.

And on I went, past Tomma Von Haeften's trampoline,
where a month ago, a young ballerina
got a hairline fracture of her ankle (on the day before
her recital) when I wasn't there to save her.
And on I went in my invisible robes,
past the overflow intake, that replaced the picturesque
sluice gate, and up the shore where the busy-body priest
moved in last summer, and there I knelt
like the Madonna at the manger
on a rock big enough to sacrifice anything on,
and I set the turtle down and mumbled
something like "live long and prosper,"
to which it must have said "amen"
before I let it go.

And shifting back to my earthly mode,
I hurried past the trampoline, and back between

the earth machines—and was pleased to notice in the distance,
Andrea DiNoto (who writes books about pressed flowers
and the Manhattan dessert scene) so I could explain to her
why I was coming out from between the rigs, even though
I'm not a sex worker. And I admit I hurried a bit, so I could
casually "run into her"—and share my tidings about
the turtle (meaning my intervention and its
miraculous deliverance). Though of course I couldn't
mention how she was standing in for the whole universe
—when she believed she was only coming from the post office
with a handful of junk mail.

But that was two hours ago, and I've just found
this other turtle on the road. With its twisted neck
pointing to the Cummings' drive, and I can hear Max inside,
barking like the seven-headed beast of the Apocalypse,
reproaching me for what I did with the other one—
surely it was an *other* one, cause from the look of *this* one,
flattened beside the pond, from which it clearly rose,
just when the earth movers (which are gone now)
were probably bearing down, I'm certain it would
never have matched my palm, not to mention
that zigzag in its lifeline, and anyhow it would have
been too heavy to lift. Though I would have tried,
anyone would have tried, with all the eyes
of the universe watching.

THE TREES

at Mass MoCA

The trees on the path to the museum
keep growing in their twisted inclinations
because it tickles us to see that when trees
are planted upside down in pots inverted in the air,
they'll send their branches in a u-turn to the sun.
Most people like the trees, the guide says, and why not?
Most people like a show. Or sideshow act.
A tiger whipped through a hoop of fire. A chained bear
in a frilly collar. A human pincushion
or a woman cut in half.

Last year on the cover of an art magazine I subscribe to,
a man was juggling a dead dog.
What ticklish complexity
when we're not sure what to make of it.
After all, it was art, and everyone likes art,
or art appreciation:
just look at us now with all our deference to the guide,
and the more he tells us, the more we put aside
our former inclinations about trees
and dogs and life and try to find accommodation

in that town where *most people* are—
you know, all those people who don't question,
who never act rude, who don't have to bring up
the downside of upside-down things,
all the people so amused by the scrawny twisted trees,
bending to our will, yet still trying to be trees—
though they're freakish now—
they're our *send-ups* of trees,
and we're laughing underneath them
with the juggler and the crowd.

Most people like the trees, the guide repeats
as the others go inside. I stay behind and ask him
which ones don't.
There are always a few, he says (he means
a few like you), who have to raise objections—
they sort of see themselves hanging there like that.
But then they go inside where everything's
avant garde, or as they say nowadays, *conceptual*—
there's nothing conventional in there,
except maybe the gift shop—

and by the time they come out, they're feeling a little
smarter, a little more enlightened, and when they see the trees,
they can laugh at them now, even tell the people coming in,
Look up at those crazy things!
They're the thing most people remember seeing here—
they always mention the trees when they come back.
You'll see yourself when you come out,
you'll feel different about the trees.
It's very sophisticated in there,
and when you come out, you'll be different yourself."

WRACKED BLUE SUITCASE

I need him to help me lift it down from the closet shelf—
the wracked blue suitcase I bought for
our honeymoon. It's got maternity clothes and baby things—
sweaters knit by his mother and a crib quilt.
And as always—even though he doesn't
ask, I feel a need to explain:
"It's got maternity things. I want to give them
to Andrea." (She's our daughter-in-law,
pregnant with their first one.)

"Okay," he says. "But only if they'll look good."
—which hits me like something falling from
a shelf when you open a closet. "Oh no," I snap back,
"they'll look ridiculous. Just like they did on me! "
Now we'll stew for an hour as we usually
do on weekends. He says I'm cranky every Sunday.
I say, "It's only because you're home. And besides,
you're testy every Saturday." "Testy,"
I repeat, "as in 'testosterone.' "

He wanted me to ride with him to the river
to see the snow—the first storm of the winter.
Instead he storms downstairs and puts
the TV on too loud. I lug the suitcase to the bed,
undo the pitted latches and lift the lid
as if I've just gotten back from a whirlwind trip
that's left me exhausted. I take out the sweaters:
the smaller two yellow—knit before
we knew—the other three blue.

Below them are the clothes I wore the year I turned
nineteen, and again when I was twenty—

keeping my jacket on in class, hoping no one
would notice, but they did, of course—
I remember being ribbed by some jackass boys in math.
I should have gotten rid of them long ago,
but every time I asked, "Do you want
another?" he'd ask me back, "Do you?"
and, as usual, we never got beyond our parrying.

But I'd forgotten about this—the tiny blue dress,
sent by Florence Smith before she heard
about our daughter. It's grayed and faded now.
And Florence is dead too. I'll give that one away,
I don't want him to see it—it might shred his
heart again. But here's the quilt he bought
when our son was born. It's frayed
from use—though not too fragile
to lend its old security to someone new.

I want to do the washing now (I even bought
some Ivory Snow). But he's calling from below
to say the car won't start—he went out and
brushed it off to kill some time,
and the battery light came on. He says he needs me
to crank it while he looks under the hood.
I leave the clothes stacked on the bed
where we've slept more than half our lives.
I get my coat from the closet. Nothing falls.

FUNNEL

Today I couldn't think of *funnel*—
though I could see them, *two* of them, nesting inside
each other on the butcher-block top of the dishwasher.
My husband was at the table with a gallon of Desert Spring
and an empty bottle from Glacier Clear—
narrow enough to fit the holder in the Volvo,
and I said, *You should use*—and the word wouldn't come—
I said, *You should use*—as the water struck the brim
and spilled down the sides and splashed to the floor
where I rushed with the sponge and said *funnel!*
As I rose up dizzy from the sudden shift of blood,
he asked me *where I'd been.*

But how could I tell him that I'd slipped into that place
we used to joke about—where all the things we can't remember
whirl around together like Dante's lovers.
Funnel, I told him, *I couldn't think of—funnel.*
Too late, he said, handing me the bottle.
On my way to the door, I tossed him the funnels—
stuck together like two kids coupling—
but my whole way on the highway
as I sipped the Desert Spring in its pose as Glacier Clear,
I kept picturing what I'd glimpsed there as I rose—
the narrow spinning room with both of us inside,
slow-dancing down the tapering of the years.

TOMMA AND SAMMY

Across the pond this morning, there's only the folding chair
with its back turned to the ice, and the pairs
of footprints that stop there in the snow—
where we saw them last evening from our window—
how she leaned toward him, brought her face
close to his, gathered his face in her hands,
slid off the seat, knelt before him,
closed her eyes. We saw her nodding—
I told my husband we shouldn't
be watching—the way she kept nodding—
nodding and talking, it was almost
too much, the way he kept looking
at her with his usual grin as if nothing
were happening before we turned away

Later in the evening, driving back from the sheep farm,
we saw them together on the road.
It was almost dark then, and she was holding
onto him by the sleeves of a sweater wrapped
around his middle. I rolled the window down—
I thought I should say something,
How's he doing? I tried with a juicy-fruit smile.
He's on his way out, she answered, she couldn't
manage more, her voice was wrung out like
a rag and he kept dragging her along,
leading her where he was going with his
usual grin, his coat, thick and golden, his
tail sweeping side to side as if
he had all the time in the world.

REAR VIEW MIRROR

If you'd seen her there, trying to rise, you'd understand
why I didn't make a sound. If you'd seen how many times
her spindly forelegs dug themselves forward, trying to
lift the stone cart of herself off her yearling flanks—
if you'd watched her head toss left and right,
searching for instructions from any corner—
if you'd seen how she finally broke through
the cowl of her pain and pulled
herself upright, you'd know
why I sat there paralyzed.

Then you'd have seen how she was denied the heady
moment given to any flimsy fawn who makes it to its feet—
how she couldn't pause a second to feel gravity
pull away from her hooves and slink back in the earth.
And you'd have stayed there with her too,
hanging onto the wheel like an exhausted god
till she tossed her death on the heap of her shadow
and hauled herself to the woods,
one leg scratching jaggedly behind her
like a lie on a lie-detector test
until she disappeared.

Only then would you have pulled apart your harness
and stepped out and seen the smashed side mirror
pressed flush against the window where your shoulder
had just been. Only then would you have
touched the caved-in door that held the
sudden wave-like thud of her wriggling spine.
Only then, Demeter-like, would you have
brushed the tufts of fur, still stuck in the
rear window gasket—and probed

a finger through the wet grassy smear
that her flailing hoof had left there.

Only then would you have figured out the strength
to go after her into the dark place where she'd gone—
to search for her and keep searching—
just the way you'd have done if you'd come to
in a dark room after labor, and found no one there,
not a cry, not a sound—like that time—
when I slid down on a sheet below a mirror—
so I couldn't watch my daughter come or go.
But this time, with the cars rushing by,
I watched in the mirror. I watched.
And I saw where she'd gone.
And I followed her in.

DEER IN THE APPLES

for Gail Gregg

A horde of apples lying in the cleft between the trees
where last night I saw two white-tails running off.
There must be fifty of them here, all plump and ruby,
where gravity rolled them down the hill into its bowl.
Though they were swollen and heavy from the feast,
one caught my scent and ran. And one is turning
brown and another's been bitten in half. I couldn't
see them in the dark. Only the white flash
of their tails. Not the way they keep transforming
in the grass till just a few are ruby at all. One is black
and one is brass. And the other one followed and ran.

They must have come back later. One already
has a worm inside its shoulder. I was nothing to fear,
not like God who sometimes walks here in the evenings,
counting his horde, sometimes dropping a handful
to watch them roll. Only a few escape the bowl:
one lies virginal and hidden in her roots, one crashed
with a leaf and stem, one ran off with the white flesh
in its mouth, and then the little deaths crept out
and left the heap of skin. I don't know where they
went later. Somewhere gravity couldn't take them
on its own. Their bellies low and heavy. The sweet flesh
softening around the bruise from the first bite.
And the other one running off when I got too close.

FORSYTHIA

Today the snowdrops are up below the bare clumps of forsythia,
which no one could tell are forsythia yet
—but now there's hope that any day there'll be
armloads of forsythia, so kids can bring them to their mothers—
like we used to do, back in the Bronx, where our neighbors
had a clump that spilled across the concrete corner.
Their house is gone—burned to the ground,
but the forsythia's still there—coming back year after year,
like a sprawling free-for-all on the vacant lot.

Being April in Old Chatham—though still not easy to believe,
the Wemples' kids have hung colored plastic eggs
in their bare magnolia. How impatient we are with nature—
wanting it to be summer before we've even seen a leaf!
And this year, after the worst snowfall in years
and all those red and orange, manufactured fears
that kept wafting up from Washington,
why wouldn't we lose hope that the world would rise again
into the shining, sheltering place it once was?

This morning I ran into Jeanie Ferrone in the post office—
she told me she had to put Jerry in a nursing home this winter.
I didn't say I put my mother in one too, maybe the cruelest
thing I ever had to do, instead I asked her if she knew
that the pretty young woman who moved in
around the corner had her baby in December:
"There was still too much snow for her to roll it in a stroller,
but she brought it into the country store—flopped in a sack
against her breast *as if it were still inside her.*"

Only three weeks ago—our fifth night in a row of five below zero,
I couldn't stand it a second longer, and snuck over to the Clarks'

to catch a whiff of anything alive.
I was barely in the barn when a lamb spilled from its mother—
hardly a pretty sight—with that floppy sack and udder,
and the two of them smeared red and yellow
like a pile of dying leaves. I panicked for a moment:
Holy Christ, what should I do? When the ewe
began to lick the wobbly thing—of course she knew!

They told me at the nursing home that my mother still won't listen
and sneaks off on her own when she has to pee.
When I visited last month, she asked me to come along,
and as she hoisted her wobbly weight from the hard embrace
of the wheelchair, I tugged the elastic down
and I could see the sad, abandoned place I came from.
They've warned her that they'll put her in the closed wing:
You–have–to–ring–the–bell! Someone–will–come–with–gloves.
She says the shame is worse than if she fell.

I'm sure when Christ rose from the dead, he must have
seem deranged—going round with all those crazy dreams to tell,
and he must have been a sight—all tangled like a nest,
with his hair in clumps and matted down.
And despite the myrrh or whatever else they'd smeared him with,
he must have smelled of sweat and death and pee.
Oh, I don't care if they say he was *radiant and risen*—
or that he'd *harrowed hell*—his body
was the body of a *man's!* If not, what good is he?

Every winter I swear I'm going to knock down that finch's nest
from the post in the corner of the side porch eave.
But each spring before I get around to it, some finch or other—
like the one up there today—has made a new nest in the old one.

My neighbor Zola used to put a stone up in her corner
to keep the birds away. Now she's gone to live with her daughter.
Last summer my mother rose up in her senility and begged me
to take her in—she said she'd *sleep in a corner of my library.*
But I rolled her away—like a pile of dying leaves.

Christ rolled the stone away—-and looking like a hippy after
a deadly weekend trip, stepped out into the scrutinizing light.
He must have panicked—it's not easy to come alive again.
When I called my mother on the weekend, she told me she's
got a boyfriend—a man on her wing who's half paralyzed.
—Can it be *true?* Can it be that after the loneliness,
after the pain and worry, and the loathing of these bodies
that we cling to till the end, we never lose our aptitude
for radiance? *I'll bring her some forsythia soon.*

THE SAME WATER

(1990)

from COMING OF AGE ON THE HARLEM

for Kathy Dros

I

My father would tie a life jacket
to a length of seaworn rope and dangle me
off the dock of the Harlem boar Club float.
A strange baptism.
Down, down into the mad rushing river,
worm on a hook, a girl of six or seven,
I am let loose among water rats, made sister
to half-filled soda cans floating
vertically home from a picnic, and to condoms
that look like mama doll socks
in the unopened infant eye.
What man would toss his child to that swill?
He who can swim across the river,
whose arms churn a feud with the current.
He thinks he can hold me from any maelstrom.
Safe on the dock, I watch my father
float on his back, from the Bronx
to Manhattan and back again.

III

The Harlem Boat Club is the man place.
My father slips down twice a week to shower,
on weekends plays a sweaty game
of four-wall ball. Outside in the garden,
I wander six years old among lilies
of the valley, Queen Anne's lace,
the shoreline irises and great climbing rose
that began as someone's potted plant.
Elmer, the muscular black cat,
drags a water rat to the front door. I follow inside
to the boat room, run my hand along
the lean flanks of polished rowing sculls,
then up the stairway, pause at the wooden roster,
the names with gold stars dead in some war.
Then the sweat smell of the lockers,
the place where they held a party
to welcome the Beatty brothers home from Korea.
Off to the side, three men
stand naked in the steamy, tiled shower.
Quiet, I sit down on a bench
beside a girl my own age, who has also come
to pretend she doesn't notice.

IV

Still my close, though distant, friend,
who sat with me in the men's locker room,
whose father had a strong right arm for handball,
whose mother and mine, embarrassed
in their forties, had pregnancies,
who accompanied me through puberty
up and down the Harlem shore,
Kathy, in your Brahmin home in Brooklyn,
you say you want to rid your sleep of those
dirty years along the river. But stop for a moment,
stop trying to make the river pass genteelly,
for there'll be no weaning from those waters.
Instead come back with me and watch
the sun glint off the rippling surface,
bearing the shore –hugging flow of turds and
condoms north to the Hudson.
You conjectured it all came from cabin cruisers
on some far-off glory ocean.
Kathy, would you have even looked
if you had known it came from humble tenements
on our Highbridge hill?
Could that one reflection
have darkened all your plans to sail?

V

"Mirror, Mirror"
was the name you gave him,
a dexterous man with a pocket mirror
who could catch the Sunday-morning sun
and flash it on our untouched child bodies.
Snow White gone haywire, Rapunzel in reverse:
"Mirror, Mirror!"
we shouted from the bridge height,
and he below us in the river park would
hold his instrument to the sky like
a sextant and calculate his grotesque angles.
Then we'd race down the ramp
just beyond his unknown reach and dive
behind the safety of a tree.
Oh God! Oh God! the heavy breathing,
ours, his, the fear, the vague desire
that was always escaped in time to
run home at one for Sunday dinner and meet our
unsuspecting fathers coming home from mass.

VIII

In Undercliff Park, below Washington Bridge,
I play stretch and toe-knee-chest-nut with
my father's pocketed army knife.
A dangerous age. Threats are cutting through the air:
the flailing depantsings, the groping bra quests for
a wad of cotton or a nylon stocking.
A dangerous age, with the deadly fear
of being found a child.
To relieve it one day, we hang a tire in a tree and
swing in packs out over the cliff edge,
until the boy beside me loses grip, and lies
below, as quiet as an infant in a lullaby.
Weeks later, we visit him at home, sign his casts
and giggle at his immature pajamas.
He lifts his mattress to show
an arsenal of thirty knives and ice picks,
and let's each girl pick a pocket lighter
shoplifted from Woolworth's.

IX

Hung by my hands above water,
I am dangled by boys from the ledge
of the Washington Bridge abutment.
Twelve years old, twelve feet from the surface,
I do not trust boys, but love their giddy danger
like a windflaw teasing with a sail.
And while we dangle, the boys hurl rocks
at the river, waiting for the splash that will leap
up to our blouses and clutch the outlines
of our forming breasts.
Soaked through, we climb the naked limbs
of a shore tree and sprawl in the afternoon sun.
Above, a boy hovers in the branches and is gone,
leaving something growing in me
that holds me separate from my friends
as we walk together to our fathers' houses,
wearing our secret scent of the river.

from THE UNMOLESTED CHILD

I

On a curbstone above a sewer I sit with my brother
while the sun gathers back its light, for
a moment intensifies, then retracts from our extending
shadows and climbs down behind the Harlem River.
Until it's gone, we'll watch the older boys contend
with sawed-off broomsticks and "Spauldeens."
Where Woodycrest intersects our street, each base is
a corner sewer. The center manhole,
the unelevated pitcher's mount. They let us sit on
third. The ball is soft and no one will get hurt.

Then from behind us, like the sudden angel
whose low reconnaissance spots the children
on the cliff, or on the slim bridge above the rapids,
he appears, the artistic nursery scene: two periled
children and the angel intervenes to save, we all
presumed, and not to push. But notice his finger.
How willfully it points at me. The same gesture which,
with matured iconology, we'll recognize in those great
depictions of unsettling authority: where it
points the lounging Adam from the comfort of
his loam. Points the tender Mary from her tranquil
broom and dust. Points the tender boy to man artillery.
I want you, says your uncle. His gesture
clearly to distrust, but I was six, and schooled toward
the comfort of strangers. And here a strange man
needing, that night, to get engaged. A man who in
a basement had lost "a blue diamond ring"
and asked me if I'd help him find it.

No matter the huddling girl on the front stoop
as he took me to the alley of my building. No matter
her plea, "Don't go with him." How matter-of-factly
he took my hand and told me, "Don't be afraid."
I was no coward: I watched stickball.
She lived around the corner, played with dolls.
My brother tagged along. But that was useless.
The stranger set his hopes on me. He squeezed
my hand, exercised his authority, gave directions
to my brother to search the yard where a cracked
couch and matching chair waited for the junkman's truck.

And I went with him. Into the second basement,
past the dark storeroom that held my grandmother's
bridal bed with pineapples on its posts,
past where the dumbwaiters waited in their walls,
to where the boiler room was darker. And there
he stood before me, positioning me, eliciting a
promise of secrecy. I still was clam. But then
an actual angel came. I grew afraid and ran.
Not knowing why. Up to my apartment
terrified, unable to explain, except, "There was a man."
My father and my uncle Marty raced down the
stairs, understanding that danger I couldn't describe.

Three weeks I had to stay inside. Then it was the police
in a car with lights and all, that took my brother and me
to the station. And there was their suspect
on the stoop of the 44th precinct, between four men and
the tall globes of justice that still face the river.
Identification was expected.
I wore my newest sundress with alphabet letters,

and was sure of almost twenty-six. They said he had
confessed. But his face seemed tanner, his hair
seemed longer. It wasn't him, I said.
My brother, undecided, sided with me. We were told
the other girl had recognized him: She, the one who
played with dolls. That night they had to let him go.

I was then, what I took for, a celebrity.
And dangerously took my friends to see the refreshment
stand his family ran under the shuttle El, near
Macombs Dam Park, just north of Yankee Stadium.
He had a history of taking small girls in the dark
and doing what I didn't know. That thing
that enraged my father so, that made my mother
whisper over the one washer in the basement laundry room.
That thing I'm sure that huddling girl
could have told. But I never saw her.
The more reliable witness, who moved away that summer.

II

Tie to tie I walk the tunnel
from its mouth on the Harlem River where we'd
broken in, to Anderson Avenue on the other
side of the neighborhood, passing under my father's
couch as he naps between his jobs
at the center of 162nd Street, where deep below,
the newly abandoned IRT tunnel bends into its darkest,
and I go: an assignation.
I spare him the expense of worry. Let him sleep
above me like the bearded God who gets
winded at our games.
I will emerge whole from beneath gas lines and
sewage pipes, and will boost myself up from the track
to the open-air platform, and there remember waiting once,
early in the morning with my mother,
and seeing the elongate spokes of the rounded iron
fence, I took it for an emblem of the sun.
Fierce and glorious. I did not apprehend
it stood against intrusion. I had taken
it as art, meaningful and useless, at an age
when I still knelt on subways and stared
into that dark and was good at taking
the occasional flicker in.

Now on the platform, corrected by
that fence, I regard it as a barrier, perceive
some loss of innocence. I wait here for a boy,
thirteen like me, sent down the eastbound track
while I walked down the west.

Pyramus and Thisbe in our jeans, we went,
though, of course, we'd never heard such things.
And now I could not hear his footfalls,
though he must have been there, just to my left.
Only the seepage water running down the walls,
the recurrent hum of hotboxes
lying in the tracks, charged still with electricity,
I was careful to step over.
A quarter way I went, looking back at what
was light. And the next quarter, at the hardly light
dying into the dark of the tunnel's bend,
and there the absolute aloneness magnified.
Only the ties counted out loud with sneaker feet kept
my heart intact. Oh how it beat until that first
barely and doubted light was real and finally there.

And I arrived too frightened to entertain desires
that my friends back on the Harlem side
would be imagining for me in this tunnel of
love, of our breakings and enterings,
where I realized there was no one else but me.
Not once did I fear for him or picture how he might
have touched something dangerous, forbidden, how he'd
been terribly burned, or how, halfway turned,
a loss of will. I knew I was abandoned: I was being
joked at. Or at least rejected. The rules were
broken. The board bumped, its pieces strewn, and I
marooned at the far end of a tunnel where he would not
come, I knew. And yet I stayed there much too long,
rummaging my head for some prescription gleaned from
teenage comic books. But there was no reference yet
to the old tunnel, where she always waits

for his arrival. The game was over early. The winter
sun soon gone from the barricaded station.
And no way back but to take that dark again.

III

It was Kathy Shackel who was caught
in the *Daily News* with a tissue at her nose.
Tomorrow she'd be explaining she simply had
a cold, but the photographer had waited for some
symbol while we stood so stoically on the steps
and the summoned baritone and tenor wove
those woeful Latins in the loft.
It was Roseanne Breen, whom we'd least expected
to be at the center of such a scene.
Roseanne Breen, only eleven, her integrity so
intact that she never played at the forbidden river
where our parents would not let us go.
Never posed there in her bathing suit
for the man who claimed he'd come from
Confidential Magazine:
That year we had thought we'd all be famous,
and so trustingly, we thumbed those seamy
pages and grew impatient and confused as we
waited to appear. Then one of us concluded:
we had been used. Maybe we had known it
since that day we so eagerly made
fools of our ourselves, smiled and moved
the way he told us, displayed our naïveté.

And now it was Kathy Shackel in the centerfold
and Margie Daniels quoted on page three for
what her mother had seen while Margie was
with me at the river, and we were endangered
only by the current, the cliff and tracks.
Coming home with sacks of groceries that afternoon,

Mrs. Daniels noticed a stain on the mosaic tiles near
the stairs, and found beneath them, a naked child
so stabbed and bloody it could not
be recognized. She thought it was her own.
What could our parents say? We who had
disobeyed, who had gone out where all their restrictions,
all their predictions of jeopardy applied,
instead were safe. And she who had dutifully stayed home
to do her homework was now inside
the box coming foot-first down the steps.
The next-door neighbor had confessed. He, the father
of two small girls, who were not there that afternoon
he made an abattoir of their living room.
But he never had entered her, he argued. Never had
penetrated her, he said. So Roseanne Breen, who was
so featured in the *Daily News* that none of us
forgets, who was eleven when we saw her last,
is unmolested still.

THE PRECARIOUS NEST

This summer I am less affected by Darwin
and the ice-action and organic production
of the Southern Hemisphere,
                                        or by his expedition
up the Santa Cruz where he saw streams of stones, fires
    made of bones,
                              and shot a condor,
  or even by his exploration of Tierra del Fuego where
in winter hunger, men ate their mothers
                                  and kept their dogs.

I am drawn more this morning to Gilbert White
making at treatise of the harvest mouse
in his own garden,
                           or becoming expert in the swallows
he flushed from the banks along his daily walk
                      in Selborne.

And I am positively at home today, early as it is, with
          John Ray, nine years observing the plants
that grew around his own door in Cambridge,
  and becoming a father, finally at fifty-seven,
coming back to a cottage in Black Notley
          and sending out his four young daughters
to collect caterpillars and butterflies
                                    for him to classify.

Here on my own narrow sun porch with its thirteen-dozen
panes of old imperfect glass, I have been
making sense of this universe.

Already this morning I have observed a robin

springing across the asphalt shingles of the garage roof,
pausing to listen, impossibly
for worms.
And the cat
hardly visible in the rose hedge.

And through these same panes I've watched
Ann Williams under the birch tree with her new
husband's shirt,
managing to thread a needle in the wind.

And Carol Wright cutting down the privet hedge
that would not leaf after the cold winter
and her divorce.

Daily I looked for the corpse of
a small starling to dry and flatten so the wind could
take it off the sloped porch
beneath the bedroom window.
But first
a heavy rain.

And I saw where, from the same precarious nest
built in the valley below the gable-dormer eave,
another hatchling,
naked and all head,
had toppled, bounced and landed in the uncut grass.
It stayed alive all night
in a box of straw outside the attic window.

But there are four, maybe even six,
unmarked eggs in a starling's nest.

Here I have been waked by the distressed
yelping of the Campbells' black dog, and
stuck on its back, caught in the act,
                                        the Bachs' black dog.
          Before sunup Saturday, and the Bachs' lights
on all night for the Sabbath.
                                        Then a neighbor running with a hose.

I now know that bees doze intoxicated
under the lime tree at the corner.
               And turning the other corner one evening
stung in the neck by a honeybee
                                                  coming from nowhere
and so unreasonable.

I have proof now that a new cat escaping down a
vine through a broken upstairs screen,
        returning that night, afraid, will cling
midway up the insubstantial strand
                    even if the back door is wide open for her.

My hands are the ones that steady the ladder.
My husband fears height.

Squirrels leap unhesitatingly from wire to wire,
          then to the shed dormer, the garage roof.
They understand foreplay.
                                             They enjoy their tails.

John Putnam, though a naval commander,
sings a sweet high formless aria when he

walks the old collie now before bedtime.
            My husband wonders if he's drinking.

Crows do not sing *down a down.*
They make a harsh din, and it's easy to think
        they see trouble coming.
But I believe they mean no harm.

                        The fierce territoriality
of our courting cardinal.
        And yet his amiable song.

The tomato vines are six feet high now, strung on
            electrical conduit pipes.
The zucchinis, gigantic,
                    pregnant, yet phallic,
        hang over into the driveway.
                    We park the car on the street.

The cardinals built in the honeysuckle
        before the new cat.
The new cat has mastered its climbing.
Objectivity is an aim of the natural scientist.

From the sun porch by moonlight, looking west
I can see, on their sun porch,
                        the Williams' brace
of exercise bikes, riderless all night.
And to the east, Carol Wright's facing the dark TV
with its solitary wheel.

Soon Nathan Bach, framed in the high shadeless
        window, will be davening in his shawl.

His search for meaning, like my own, goes on,
not leading to his loss of freedom,
or anything else's.

Whatever we prayed to once
is there outside the porch panes, still
                                answering or ignoring our prayers.

There is always some weed that the garden loves.

THE GROTTE DES INFANTS

I

Seventeen years and again the wet sheet,
a stain from something given way.
    A thing had whimpered somewhere in that
room. My legs bound to metal stirrups,
I could not see, and there was no one
to tell me, but called your name and knew
which name to use.

Was it the emptiness I was in that moment,
strapped open in communion with the wide, dark
gapes between the stars. Did I hope
by that calling to spare you what
     few things I could: the futile
rib, the womb of oceans drained by each moon,
the lacteal sacs borne all those years
                    for that whimpering.

I was the first to say your name. The first
to ask you to keep silent.

II

After the first emergence. Brought back together
again. Again. The blood to the sheet.
    A nail in your sole. The hand caught
in the door. The knee sliced nudging
a fish tank across the back seat of the car.

Beneath the curtain that last time, we watched
blood drop on the tiles and splash into smaller
drops. A man on the other bed had cut
his wrists, and we stopped the usual joking
and watched the black shoes of cops and the dropped
                    gauze and the reflection
on the cabinet glass. He once had been
the luckiest man alive, he said.

Now you are in his bed. Teeth in the gauze. And I
on the metal stool, watch the stain soak from
the center, crust and hold a little till
it must be replaced.
Some boy has tracked your face. His cleats notched in
your chin, your lips, the bridge of your nose.

It is my last year for your emergencies.
You mumble, "Good."
Is there nothing more
to spare you? Scalpels or needles? Two dozen kinds
of thread, named and numbered in cardboard
boxes on the wall.
What will it be next year?

Rubble. The repeating sound
of fire. The dislocated bones.

III

Last night in Esther's kitchen I saw
a photo from the Times. A Turkish woman in
Narman with five small sons laid out on the ground,
in the gentlest curve and her arms curved
above them, one elbow crooked just a bit, just so,
as she knelt on the stone.

And all the balance of the scene. And her mouth
open in communion with all dark
spaces.

If it had been art, someone would
have said: Too many. There should be just one or
two. Or someone would have thought the fractured earth
too obvious or uncontrolled.
But no one was there to sketch the scene for her.
And what did the woman know?

The earth did
it. Cracked and topped her village. And she laid out her
sons as best she could. Not knowing that
if she were an artist, she might
have saved most of them.

IV

A collagist once, I lacerated things.
Recombined and reinvented them. Set them off,
the visuals composed, the contents skewed.
Humor. Shock. Dispassion. The last laugh.
How young I was.
And how removed.

But somehow, inexplicable, from that fierce cutting,
I saved those pictures, Madonna and child, always
a the moment that is also Pietá. When the lap
or ground has caught what is given, broken and taken
in the instant continuum that she knows the first
time the head wobbles on her arm.
The most classical and primitive of configurations:
the triangle of mother and child and what she broods.

Picture the head, small and abraded, pressed to the
olive sari that waits as it finishes its dying
on the road from what was East Pakistan. Or the
dehydrated flanks framed by the white cotton mantle
that falls from shoulders down the useless breasts in
the Sahel, in Upper Volta.
                                        Or the hands that sponge
what they could not spare the deformed limbs
in Minimata, in Kyushu.
Even the girl at Kent State become
a mother to someone's crumpled son whose face
leans to the curb, away from what gave out
on the concrete drive.

I told Esther I could not take another picture.
Who can save any of them anymore?
This week a warehouse in Dover fills with wood from
Lebanon. Not cedar. It is pine wood. And boxes in bright
three-colored cloth come up from the beaches of Grenada,
come into the bass tones at the podium where the
air vibrates from hollow brass. Where a small triangle
is given. To be embraced to the breast. A folded flag.
Something to be saved.
We have sons that age, Esther said.
We know it would not be enough.

V

Who is she, the nurse asks.
Not even addressing me. I answer for you.
The cracked teeth and lip split clear, needing
no exegesis. Does she expect you to look down
and say in a calm and Galilean tone, "Behold."
    She scrutinizes me for rings, wrinkles,
growth signs. The old tree. Knobbed. Gnarled. Cut down.
At last I'll do.

At first she thought I was your lover.
And you, too tall to have this mother anymore.
Now the same vain flatteries we hear in
theaters and department stores. She leaves you
on the bed. Mud stripes your cheekbones, blackens out
your nose. You terrified a child as we passed through
the waiting room. Now it is bedtime and I am out
of stories.

                Who is she, I ask the cabinet
door. She was the green bell pepper
full of seeds, cut open on the board.
She was the dinghy-boat on whose
spine you rocked to shore. She was the vault
above the altar intoxicated by incense and
nonsense. Her ribs gone to rafters now like
the starved Buddha. She finds nothing left to give.

VI

Now the quiet, light domestic scene. The blue-green
cloth unfolded, spread over your scalp, pulled down
across your forehead, eyes and nose.
A man is threading a needle and I
am asked to leave.
I, who have been there since
you were called down into existence.
I who was cast and drilled in the drama on
the square white stage whose yielding center
has pulled you and everyone into it.
Twenty I was. Too young for absolute expectancies.
I demanded nothing be given. But I did not know I would
be asked to go so soon.

Where is the plastic box, whose indented
gold letters say "teeth," where I keep
the four pulled out that summer in Stroudsberg,
still with their crooked undissolved roots.
Today it will have six. And it will not be enough.
Not ever enough. Not enough when Julia's sister
had her son back from Saigon. Only teeth.
She could see what they carried was
too light. What she had carried . And she could not
be deceived.

The doctor talks of college as he pulls.
Nine stitches. In the hall I count the sound of
scissor clips. Hear you mumble to his questions.
Incomprehensible. But more than you've given me today.

Once here, years ago, I asked you to be silent.
Were you so old even then, that you remember?

VII

In the Grotte des Infants, among
the caves of Grimaldi,
were buried the bodies of son and mother.
Cro-Magnons. Now specimens. He, much taller,
kneels with his chin beside her ear. And
the beads that were his cap have fused to his
skull as the bones went bare. And see her hand
under his chin. Her other hand
with a bracelet of the same beads.
Head by head. Kneeling beneath her
where they have gone together.

Oh what would people say if they
were alive, or had a scrap of flesh left,
flesh that formed, separated, stank
and merged again.

VIII

On the wall the doctor shows the pictures.
Frontal. Parietal. Lateral. Occipital.
Life size. The grinning child.

The same grinning child who once
saluted his father's camera with a wave from
under water. The child
who posed in the ersatz classroom for
the fourth-grade photographer and smiled there
with the flag and autumn scene for his out-of-town
grandmothers. The child who stopped
mid-step when the flashbulb went
in the living room where he danced with
the percussionist's deaf daughter.
                                        The child
who dropped in the net and was preserved
in muck today for the high-school paper. A save.
Bloody and grinning. Still grinning.
                                        No sign of
pain now in the two hollow orbits beneath
the fleshless tori, or along the sagittal suture
where the soft plates shut, where no dura mater,
no pia mater shows. No pain now
through the back, through the foramen magnum
where no mother should be asked to go, where I see
again the same dark opening I know, the gaping
space I thought I'd filled.

LARKSPUR

for Sheila Dudek

Warm weather, and the couple who've moved in
across the street are raking. He wears a turban.
She a pair of jeans. I like their laughter
and their daughter, a small blond thing with
a dirty spoon, who on Sunday left larkspur
in my garden where they'll never grow.
She dismissed my talk on shade, said
she'll watch them from her window.
A flat, unstable star, her hand spread.
I obliged her. Tapped her packet till she'd
counted four and saw them: not hapless bits
of matter, but pink and purple as their picture,
the ribbings of her sweater. She broke
a clod. Dumped them. Tamped it with
a sneaker. Repeated her unsupported
hopes, and had me cross her.

On Saturday, among foiled mums, routine
baskets filled with leaves, a fake bird and one
true, tall spike of larkspur, I found my
son , stretched out with a girl, his
sleeve against her I.V. Thirty metal staples
marked the furrow. They took a kidney and
the thing it grew: Five pounds. Pink.
Ripe. And overdue. Some starry cells,
they say are in there still.
So who's to pull this long boy from
her bed? A wise nurse. Or a mother.
This girl has neither. His dirty socks
accuse me of delinquencies. Of years when I

ignored their rumpled sheets, their washy
dreams, and waved them off to school. At noon
my husband crosses to the Rundel Library.
The texts abstruse, worded for doctors.
He phones me the statistics over lunch, varieties
that sound Linnean as the Burpee seeds we'd
meant to order. I too was twenty once.
They laid him on my chest. A five-pound bunch.
With no instructions, and little time to watch.

THE SAME WATER

Sooner or later each kid who fishes
in uneventful water
where the bob only bobs and is not pulled under
will imagine the sameness of heaven
and by lunchtime will realize in his boredom
that all water converges
and must be shared by everyone.
He will see that his line extends thirty-six thousand
feet down into the Mariana Trench
and that in a hundred
million years, or maybe a lot sooner,
the waves licking his knees will slick the back
of a sixty-foot whale shark
slumbering in an equatorial sea.
It's a lure for any fisherman.

Even Jesus with his wet soles and
perfumed ankles wrapped in yellow hair, walking,
grew gradually aware how barnacles
bleed the flesh and harrow our hulls.
He knew then, how few were saved.

Olav, my uncle, twice torpedoed and preserved,
a merchant seaman who could tell you how to float,
would tell you how it's easier to go under.
So much has gone under this July.

A fall has paralyzed a lifeguard
in the Town of Rye on Oakland Beach.
Headfirst
off his watchtower.
Eighteen, with a crushed vertebra.

And who is safe to swim now?

In Winona Lake, in Warsaw Indiana, even a magician's died.
He was handcuffed and chained and
                                                            jumped in the water.
   Twenty-three,
                              and his magic failed him.
Yet all the water keeps converging,
demonstrably downstream,
                                                  or at least in the clouds.

When Carol, once my neighbor, came today for lunch
    she told how she still sees her father
                                                                  padding clumsily
up the long pool outside their Cold Spring Harbor home,
under the watertight weight
                                                  of a brass helmet, trailing
an air pipe, a stream of small bubbles,
in twenty-pound boots, and eighty pounds of lead
belted at his waist.
                                        And how his face in its clear, round
portal changed, blued and grimaced
while her legs dangled in the pool.
                                                          Nine years old
when he called to her with his hand
slowly, repeatedly, through the water
to come and release the belt as he had shown her.
Frightened, she did not come.
And she did not leave him.

And it was the same water when my husband saw his
father in the morgue. Three months

  in the Harlem River, where it coves and the young
crews from Columbia pass, in their swift
sculls, the painted "C" on the bluff wall.
  The first day of spring,
                                    his head crushed and some
of it gone.
We slept with a light till summer.

But still divers only dream of finding riches
in the wrecks off New Jersey, where the surf
                        can beat men crazy,
off Ocean City where we all must go
to line the boardwalk and watch them go down
                                                                and hopefully
come up
          with something.
Three thousand cases of Japanese curios
  lie in the *Sindia*'s hold.

And there or where you are, all the water's joining yet.
Ineluctable, even as we make for shore,
                    it capsizes our pleasure boats, yields gory
stuff in the stomachs of tiger sharks, warps our
bindings, or wraps our London Fogs in odd, fishy smells,
                       Year after year, it bobs our bobs,
up to our knees
                         in the same water.

The same water that brings whales back to Provincetown
  where tourists sing their "thar she blows."
And at the wheels, the scions of whalers
                   pursue descendant whales,

spot the spout, the fluke that bucks
and descends
before they can think too much
or follow.

Whales are not saddled with ghosts or animosity.

The tide reverses itself twice daily.

Some days the fishing is better.

Footprints grow fainter the father away from the pool.

This summer Carol has moved to Long Point. The new
town houses off Ontario Street. "If it is time
for a change," the prospectus said.
And it is time.

Her wall of window faces the water.
The lighthouse with its round beacon, so close
she could toss a rope to it.
Or walk across the little inlet
to reach it, when it freezes.

MY FATHER'S LAST WORDS DURING THE BREEDERS' CUP

I think I like Cruget on Palace Music in the mile
though Rousillon, the favorite, will be
hard to beat. And I won't care that it is
Guerra on Cozzene. Cruget will place,
and by the time he is disqualified for
blocking in the stretch, I will have died.
With the bed up now, I can make out the sign
over the OTB. Earlier I meant to send
the boy across. But, maybe it's late repentance,
I'll watch it uninvested on the screen, here in
intensive care, where the TV hovers like the Lord,
and the numbers of my heartbeat flash in green.

So it's Pearson, dragging the curtain up the rod.
That means it's time. All wagers in. He's signaling
my wife and kids to leave. But I'll keep
my horses floating across the ceiling while I
sign some other paper I can't read.
He'll open up some vein. There'll be another tube.
I remember how Elaine's horse, bloated on apples, flew
across the field, the tubes they'd brought to
pump him, streaming from his nose.
All right. I'll go. Before the big race. Before
Piggot rides his last at Aqueduct today: half deaf,
he'll go direct, ignore their blame and praise.

Last night I saw they had a party for the Cup up at
the Museum of Natural History. The celebrities and owners
dressed in tuxes, and waltzed in the Hall of Ocean Life.
There was turf on the floor. Fences and a barn door.

And green felt covering the fish as if they
weren't there. So let it be green turf for me,
some small patch on this island I will share with
Belmont, Aqueduct, and Roosevelt. But let it be out here
where the old potato farms and turned to paddocks
for the thoroughbreds. And before I rest my head let
Bill Tarpey drive from West Point to say how fast I was,
how crowds coming from Yankee games would stand
at Macombs Dam Field to watch me throw, and let his
brother Marty remind them, too, how I raced
under the Harlem River, farther than anyone could go.
Then let my wife be proud. She who took me with
my gambling debts, who saw me gamble here and lose,
let her count a hundred wreaths of flowers.

QUEEN OF THE MIST

(1999)

Queen of the Mist is a book-length work telling the story of the first person to go over Niagara Falls in a barrel.

These fifteen poems offer an abridged version of the story. The numbers give their position in the six-section, forty-eight-poem original.

INITIATION [I-I]

Sealed in my barrel,
with an anvil's weight beneath my feet,
I sailed upright,
listened for Holleran's tap—
twice on the lid staves
—then they cut me loose.
I rode low, scraped the bottom stones,
clipped a rock, caught the current.
In a moment I was at the brink,
thudding on the cusp—
pitching forward, breathless, blind—
from a womb
of my own making.

Niagara!—over me!—*under* me!—
I spilled into it from every pore,
lost myself
in the blackness of its roar.
Something opened—grew wide—tore—
till every part of me was new:
Brain. Eyes. Tongue
—down to the wet soles in my shoes.
I took my measure, checked my sex
and, pleased with what I'd made,
I slapped my back between the blades
and took a breath
of consciousness.

THE PHENOMENON [I-3]

The church bells rang on both sides of the river,
spreading rumors of "a miracle."
And from everywhere they came to have a glimpse of it
—scrambling down the gorge
as if it were the final call at the final resurrection,
and then they saw me—
a puzzling phenomenon:
a woman, short and plain—and only slightly bruised,
moving dizzily among them
like a fly hatched by mistake in the winter sun.
I saw their puzzled looks—
and wondered if they'd like to put me back!

I had done what all the scientists had said no one could do
—I was, in fact, the first to ever try.
And though I lied about my age, I was really sixty-three,
I was plump and nearly grey
when they poured into the gorge to look at me—
a baffling phenomenon:
I was not a beauty or a man, yet there I was,
the center of attention.
Someone asked about my college degree,
they started questioning my intentions.
Then Russell, my manager, gave the crowd a little wave
—and handed me a *single* red carnation.

Now they waited for me to regale them:
they asked for details, observations—
"*gory* details!" someone called (he must have seen
my drooping shoulder and my head bruise),
but I was still too stunned to speak—
I was a difficult phenomenon.

Yet I tried to find some words that would please them.
But how could I *begin* to explain
what had occurred in that barrel
—that had changed my life into my *own* possession?
So I looked into their eyes, I even found a smile,
and I told them, *I am alive.*

DOING CARTWHEELS [I-4]

I know you're wondering how I thought of such a thing—
an educated woman, at the beginning of the twentieth century,
and if I had a Muse to illuminate my story,
you might see the hand of Fate—
but all I can tell you on my own
is that my plan *was born of Necessity.*
I was in Bay City, Michigan,
a lumber town on the Saginaw
—in a studio with gaslights
and a bargain-priced hardwood floor.
And since it was a time of promise and prosperity,
I found credit for a secondhand piano.

I had a hundred students from the finest families
and taught ballroom dance and manners, fall through spring
—culminating in a coming-out cotillion
into lumber-town "society."
But then the number dropped to seventy.
They were strained by the expense
of year-round classes,
their requisite corsages and livery coaches,
and embroidered satin gowns,
shipped C.O.D. from Chicago and New York.
So I modified my theme to "rhythmic dance"—
they got by in local taffeta for their seasonal recitals.

And when enrollment fell to fifty,
I gave them "Summer Promenades" and "Winter's Eve Tableaux"—
where they could learn some simple movements in a week—
and stroll about the streets
—or pose as the Fates or Muses (in homemade crepe paper gowns).
When the count had dropped to thirty,

I switched to acrobatics. (I had studied physical culture
and was a certified instructor
—the girls were quite amazed to see my cartwheels).
But my rent was overdue, I'd run up a tab for food,
I needed winter boots,
and enrollment fell to twenty.

I held an evening tea-and-social for the parents.
I showed them my diploma from the Normal School in Albany.
I told them where I'd taught and been a principal.
Why, I could tutor *every academic subject*
—teach them French or Spanish—or instrumental music.
Why I could even teach their daughters *proper English.*
—Couldn't they see them,
with improved elocution,
moving comfortably in "fashionable society"?
But when I asked them what they wanted
—how I could serve them or their children,
someone asked, *"Wouldja demonstrate yer cartwheels?"*

A WOMAN'S OPTIONS [I-5]

I walked in my despair along the Saginaw—
listening to the water toss itself against the darkness,
watching it rush headlong on the same purposeless course
it had been following for seven thousand years.
Now and then, a human thing—
a piece of fence, a box or barrel—
bobbed to the surface, was whirled and upended,
battered from bank to bank—and kept on going.
I watched it twist beneath the same bruised moon
that was inching through the same forsaken sky
it had inched through fifty million times
with its borrowed light and empty mythologies.

I could see it was the ending of a story—
where a deluded mortal wakens from a dream.
My teaching days were gone—along with Saginaw "society."
Even if I placed an advertisement,
or paid a boy to put my card in every door on every city street,
at last I understood: it was now the *twentieth* century,
and no one wanted waltzes, no one set a value on civility.
I saw the options left me—
the options of all single, destitute women over forty:
I could turn to poorhouse charity
or keep my self-sufficiency by scrubbing pots and privies
—and spend my nights doing other people's laundry.

But another option spread itself before me:
I looked down at the river—the current that could not refuse me
—and in its lethal invitation was the *one endurable* future I could see.
I could see where it would drag me:
Up to Saginaw Bay and down through Lake Huron.

Down the St. Clair, the Detroit, and into Lake Erie.
Two hundred miles more till I reached the Niagara—
and there I saw what I'd become:
a splinter of wreckage, a shard of myself,
a thing beyond caring or meaning.
—And I wanted to *be* that—
I climbed the rail, stretched my arms—and *gave* myself to it.

How can I explain how something lifted me then—
not only off the railing and up from the river—
but held me hovering above a chasm more luminous than heaven.
And when it set me down again,
soaked to my skin, with my hair dripping down my neck,
I knew I'd seen—Niagara Falls.
Niagara!
I had seen it once before
from my father's apple wagon, the autumn I turned seven.
I remember how I dropped my apple from my hand
as my eyes climbed its brilliant plume of mist,
rising effortlessly to the light—

And how the rim of the Horseshoe came in sight,
and from its roiling crucible, the sound—
—the *sound!*—as a billion simultaneous poundings
struck like thunder every knot down my spine.
I had no words then to describe its impact,
no means to distinguish its energy from mine.
It imparted everything to me
(a farmer's daughter from Auburn!)
—It entered me—vision and concussion,
and coded itself in my nerves and my brain.

And now in Bay City, on a rail above the Saginaw,
it revived itself: A *ledge* where I could leap—to *save* my life.

FIAT! [I-7]

Then—like the Virgin Mary—
I was quickened:
I got down on my knees
and spread two lengths of pattern stock
and began to sketch a shape:
I rounded it and tapered it,
added and erased
—till I knew it would accommodate my size.
In the morning, I bought some cardboard sheets.
And, cutting them, with a care I usually saved for silk,
I had my second skin
of cardboard barrel staves.
I laced them piece to piece with twine
—then crawled inside the thing.

After, I sent a boy to fetch the cooper.
I seated him in the parlor with a cup of tea.
I didn't look up as I talked,
but stared at the gold rim of my cup—
my hand trembling
—not from fear—
but from the excitement of hearing my plan materialize.
When he finally understood,
he stormed through the door (with a trail of oaths
and all my neighbors' eyes).
But three days later,
once I'd pawned my father's wedding-gift gold watch,
I called him back
and watched him change his mind.

And then I got to supervise his workers:
I picked each piece of thick Kentucky oak.

I held it to the light,
examined it—for warps, knots, insect bores
—the slightest sign
of any imperfection.
I oversaw the oiling and the joining,
the welding of the hasp and iron bands.
I satisfied myself
with the articulation of the hatch.
I ignored their laughter.
I admired the lines of my vessel—
the contours (resembling mine)
—of the thing they said would be my tomb.

"SHE'S COMING!" [III-I]

A crowd flowed onto the Suspension Bridge.
Another onto Prospect Point.
A third onto the Three Sisters Islands
—all along the railings in the gorge.
Across the river, a thousand more poured down to Table Rock.
And up the shore, a hundred others—
men, women and children—
stood by the dock at Truesdale's cottage, waiting to see me off.
There were no clouds that morning,
and so much light it seemed ten suns were whirling
as I stepped into the skiff—in a tossing sea of handkerchiefs—
and waved to them (while Russell blew a kiss)
amidst the general hurrah.

Then we set out—with Truesdale straining the tiller
against the single, headstrong sail—
and Billy Holleran, a strong, strapping boy, manning the furious oars.
The barrel rode upright behind us, bucking to run its course
—and was jerked back to correction by the stern instruction of our rope.
A quarter way out, we stopped on an island where I changed my clothes:
no hat or dress now, but a blouse left open at the throat,
and a skirt hemmed just below the knee.
I made them turn away while I backed in through the rim—
then they fastened down the lid,
rolled me to the shore,
turned me upright—
pushed me in.

Four boats now. And behind the first,
the towed barrel, weighed down with me—
yet still intractable.

And in the last, a cameraman recording every stroke
as they rowed a mile across to the Point of No Return—
where the river starts to churn,
and a sailor knows he'd better bend his back
—or else go over.
There they knocked. And cut the rope.
They must have pulled hard then to turn themselves south,
but I went north—(a half mile more before I'd reach the brink).
I careened and spun. Once it tossed me clear up out of the water.
I went unbidden—and unwelcome—where it rushed me.

I wished I could have watched from some place overhead
and heard the voices racing down the shore—
passing on the message—
dock to island, island to rock, rock to bridge:
"She's coming!"
I would have liked to see them turn their heads—
wave after wave, as each new group heard the murmur
and craned their necks to catch a glimpse.
I'd have liked to see the trolley racing down the shore,
and the incline railway rushing down the gorge
—so the ones who'd waved from Truesdale's dock
could be standing on the rocks below the Falls,
looking up—to see if *anything* would come.

DESCENT [III-2]

Over the Horseshoe's lap I dropped
—through the watery shrouds that clung about its knees.
It rolled me over and grasped me in its jaws
and was determined to have me.
My neck was lashed. My brain tore.
I felt it skin me like a hare.
Its fingers settled on my throat,
and had it asked me
to surrender to its roar
of blackness, its blaze
of nothingness,
I'd have yielded
for any drop
of mercy.

Then I glimpsed, through the turbulence,
my father and mother who had died when I was twelve.
Once I mourned them beyond recovery,
and here they were—signaling me to come.
And there was my young husband—
dead since I was twenty—
and in his arms,
our baby—
trembling and whimpering
—as on the day he left me.
I wanted to go with them.
I wanted to console them.
I wanted *them*
to *save* me.

But then I fell into the whirlpool,
and my veins and arteries unwound.

My cord rocketed from its stack of bones.
My joints unlatched. My pulse
spread out through space. Every atom of me
dispersed—to a place I couldn't name.
I moved in and out of it like breath—
expanding and contracting
through its infinite rings,
until only a single
cell of me remained.
and dropped
like a pebble
to the bottom.

RETURN [III-3]

Awakening in that dark,
where maybe nothing was,
what an effort it took
to keep conscious of the task of being.
Everything around me was shifting
—every surface, wet and slippery—
each motion I made
was a new one:
uncertain and imprecise,
rehearsed and repeated
until I got it right
and could keeping going.
Once I slipped, and, falling,
was certain I heard something whimpering.
I pushed myself toward it
—stumbling headfirst over things
that groped
to stay me as I passed.

Finally, where the water ended,
something soft spread itself before me,
and I might have stopped and slept forever
—if a crack of light had broken through then
—and nudged me forward
—to push myself through
before it closed again.
It was narrow. It hurt. It seemed impossible—
until I saw the child,
lying with her knees up to her chin.
I worried she was dead
because I'd come so slowly.
I bent to stroke her hair

—and felt my fingers
cradling my own head.
And so—
I brought myself
to life.

DEBRIEFING [III-4]

Sealed in my barrel,
I was awakened by a jolting flash of light
as something hurled me from the whirlpool
—and I saw a hand
(moving beneath the monogrammed initial on my cuff).
And when its fingers floated down and touched my skull—
I felt a throbbing pulse—I knew I was *alive!*
And though I tossed on for a hour—
afraid that I would die—
in the hellish cauldron below the Falls
—already I'd been saved:
I had gone to the grave and found *myself* there.
So I waited (and I prayed)
till the thunder snapped again
—and a grappler snagged a strap
and dragged me in.

At first they couldn't budge the lid—
I was frantic, gasping, breathless—someone ran
to get a saw—then everyone was shouting, "She's alive!"
The church bells rang as I took a wobbly step.
Their hands reached out to touch me.
A child ran to hug me
—but her mother pulled her back.
They started to inspect me: was I *"launching some crusade?"*
A woman yelled, "Your mother must be spinning in her grave!"
Then Russell stepped forward, gave the crowd a little wave,
and handed me a single red carnation.
Now reporters asked for "detailed observations."
(A preacher wanted "secret revelations.")
They didn't know what to do with me

—And I had thought
that they would *praise* me.

I was hurt. And wet. And cold. I said I wanted to go home.
And when their brief elation had slumped to disappointment,
they brought me to my bed,
piled on the blankets,
and wedged hot water bottles, up and down my sides.
I lay as still as a cadaver, grateful for the rest
—until a trio of surgeons
began to probe my torso (maybe looking for a gash
to put their hands in—so they could prove, as in the gospel,
that I truly *was* alive.
They flexed and poked me for an hour
(at least they didn't use their knives),
gave me plasters, ointments, pills
—left a little stack of bills—
and pronounced me "fit"—
for the reporters.

Already jotting, they took their places at three sides of my bed—
flattering me, coaxing me to speak,
and when the words refused to come,
one brought his head close to my cheek
and whispered, "We're all in this together now."
But how could I explain what I'd found below Niagara—
how I saw my soul in slumber
—how I struggled for its life.
So I described instead—
how I bumped across the rapids,
and how I tumbled down the Falls:
"And as you see," I said, "I'm still alive."

But when I read their faces, all I saw was disappointment.
And at last I understood what they had wanted,
but by then I'd gone too far to change my story
—and tell them I was dead.

VISIO BEATIFICA [III-7]

That night as I left the Pan American Exposition,
I couldn't help but see (in the glow of all the electric lights),
that Indian maiden—"the Maid of the Mist."
She was naked and slender,
with long brown hair and delicate features
—and in urgent need of rescue
as she plunged from the brink in her flimsy canoe.
She was prominent and everywhere—
the symbol for the Exposition
—on handbills—on posters—on banners!
—an available measure to compare me to.
And so I understood what I was up against—
and why everyone, who'd stood in line to meet me,
had met me with that same glazed disappointment
I used to see in children's eyes,
all those years I taught in schools
—whenever I would try to teach some truth.

But how easily I could enthrall those same bored children,
by leaving truth behind and opening a book of fairy tales—
where every kingdom has a pretty, sleeping princess.
—And every boy could dream how he would save her
(and every girl resolved to go to sleep).
"The great Niagara has been conquered by a woman!"
The headlines had given me away,
and now no man (or boy) could save me anymore.
I had thrown away my frailty and my fear—
my most appealing "female traits"
(I had lost my youth and beauty long before)
—now everything about me was a liability.
My old invisibility fell from my face:
I, Annie Taylor, turning gray and thick in the waist,

had dared to do a thing that no man had ever done.
I stood before them like a Gorgon
and turned them into stone.

Yet inside me, something glowed
like a tuft, ripped from the hide
of the golden fleece!
I had gone into the grave to get it—
and after struggling back with it,
I asked only that it be acknowledged—
that my *deed* be acknowledged—
that my *life* be acknowledged.
Yet they dismissed me when I said I was *alive*
—that I was *living* proof
that *they* could do
the thousand things they longed to do but never dared.
I stood before them
with the weeds still tangled in my hair,
and the silt still dripping from my nose—
But no one looked beneath my surface
—to see something that might not repel them.

THE WINDOW [IV-1]

Two weeks after I had stunned the world
—had forced Niagara to pause in its course to regard me—
Two weeks after I'd engraved myself on history
—I sat in a vacant store in Bay City, Michigan,
telling my story for a dime.
For fourteen days, the pieces gathered,
and though the puzzle wasn't yet complete,
it seemed that Russell, with his casual extravagance,
had squandered everything—before we'd even left Niagara!
Everything I'd earned was gone,
and each morning in the mail, came another dunning note,
and so I sat behind that glass all afternoon—
hardly the sleeping beauty—more like someone
in a pillory—or a debtor on exhibit in her jail.
I answered all their questions—which were all the same:
"What did it feel like?"
"Were you awake?"
"Would you do it again?"
"How much money did you make?"

What I'd done had once seemed larger than the world
—but now I doled it out in ten-minute intervals
so each of them listening
could dispense it in ten seconds to the next one in the crowd.
The Falls shrunk as they carried off its pieces
—until it seemed a small, scarred rock,
annoyingly dropped on some farmer's new-plowed field.
I should have known it was *not* a thing for words.
Maybe a painter could have got it whole,
could have told about the motion and the light,
could have hinted at the moment of creation—
that collision of hell and paradise

—could have said what I felt inside
(and still feel now)
—though I could never find the words for it.
And still I had to tell it. And tell it again. And tell it tomorrow. And tell it the next day.
And the next week down in Flint
—where Russell had found another empty store.

CRAWL ON ALL FOURS [IV-7]

Please don't misunderstand me:
not for once moment did I expect the kind of accolades
that belong to those who'd reached the Pole,
or found the Nile's source,
of the cure for some disease
or large-scale human misery.
But I was a heroine—even if a minor one—
by any definition.
I was the *only* one who'd taken on Niagara—
a test of human will—
a feat the whole word said
no man will ever do
—And so I kept a naïve hope
that *someone* might want to hear my story.

In every city—every town with a tent—
crowds lined up daily to listen to the men
who could tell them how it was
to swim the Channel—
or explore the jungle
—or spend a week on a flagpole in a field!
There was a man at the Exposition
who was getting nightly raves
for describing how he'd
lived inside a cave for half a year
(his wife brought him his meals and did his laundry),
and through his silence and discipline,
he had found the *fourth* dimension
—and everyone was lining up to hear him.

One evening during dinner in the canteen,
Russell pointed out a man,

who had crossed the Brooklyn Bridge
"by walking up its girders on his hands."
The man sat down beside us
(it struck me this was planned)
and told me that he's been to see my show—
And if I'd take "some kind advice,"
he could "blow a little life" into my act.
He'd suggested I should add some song and dance:
he'd composed a tune himself—
on the Brooklyn Bridge, of course
—but for "a small reward,"
he'd set it with some words about the Falls.

And if my legs "still had some shape,"
I should hike my skirt and pantomime my fear:
He rolled his trousers
up his calves to help him demonstrate
—then let go—*a shrill falsetto*
(that stunned me so I couldn't' even laugh).
"I've been thinking," Russell said, as if on cue,
"then she should get down on all fours—
and crawl into her barrel
—and tell her tale from there."
And everyone around us
(with their elbows on the table,
and their supper in their mouths)
nodded to endorse this *grand idea.*

SOLO FLIGHT [V-7]

This time I sought no references or opinions,
but consulting with myself,
I had a sudden (if belated) intuition
—that the *obvious* person—
for the position of my manger
—was *me*.
After the briefest possible interview
(over a breakfast of blueberry pancakes),
I assigned myself the duty
of calling on a scholarly man, much in demand
for his lectures on graphology, phrenology, and hypnotism
(and for his solo demonstration of the dance of the honeybee).
Recognizing "my potential"
—and seeing how, as a woman, I would never eclipse him,
he gave me, free of charge, a list of all his contacts
in Boston, Philadelphia, and New York.
And though he said I shouldn't hope
to net the fees *he* could command
(being a man with a Ph. D. in literature
and a course in natural philosophy),
I could probably—as he had done—
"make a living of the podium."

I started in Boston
where I appeared behind a seven-year-old farm boy,
who, from "his prior life in Caesar's army,"
could stand and recite "Omnia Gallia est"
—up to the part of Vercingetorix's death—
without ever stumbling on a line.
Next came a thirty-year-old woman,
whose spine "being aligned with the earth's magnetic poles,"
could read the minds of people in remote parts of the globe

—like the Emperor of China,
who, it seemed, spent all his nights
cheating at mah-jongg with his wives.
Last, was an eighty-year-old man,
whose dental plates
"conducted waves
from Western Union telegrams,"
which he rapped out on a table,
while "a former Pinkerton official,"
translated every dash and dot:
COME QUICKLY   STOP
THE CHILDREN HAVE JUST
SHOT THE MAID

My audiences were, for the most part, "attentive"
—my act was, by intention, less inventive than the rest:
A few listeners seemed genuinely inspired—
usually there were women, and most of them were wives.
"Just look at *me*," I'd say:
"Small and frail, aren't I proof
that you can stand up to the things that frighten or inhibit you,
and do the things you *truly* want to do before you die?
You'll do things so much greater than I did
—and much more *needed* by this world.
And if at times you feel afraid,
then just imagine
that I'm standing by your shoulder."
To end my lecture, I'd lay my hand on my barrel.
and ask them all to rise—
and say along with me, *"I am alive."*
After the applause, I'd sometimes see a few men glowering.
Once, one shouted from the rear,

"I met Annie Taylor in New York last year
—a lovely young girl—with pretty blond hair.
Madam, if you have a shred of honor,
admit you're an *impostor!*"

IMMUTABILITY CANTO [V-8]

Each winter I lectured in the large cities—
in halls and auditoriums—
in church basements
and the parlors of wealthy patrons.
Often with hucksters, charlatans, and fabricators.
Sometimes with orators and educators.
—And occasionally with reformers
whose subjects were so serious and urgent
that I yielded them a portion of my time
—giving up an evening's chance to sell my postcards
(though every coin meant my survival till the spring).

It was a grace to realize *(finally)*
that it really didn't matter half as much as I had thought—
what my listeners said or did.
Let them heckle me. Or walk out in the middle.
But maybe with some luck (either mine or theirs),
a few of them might be moved in some way—
not even remembering who it was,
or what she might have said
that had helped them change the world for the better
(or *at least* had left them more equipped
to deal with the immutable misery of it).

How good, I thought, to be over that fever of old pride
that had made me crave
to be acknowledged for what I'd done—
I felt no loss to find it gone.
And sloshing through the snows of dismal cities,
all those winters, I went more easily,
once I realized I wasn't dragging it behind me
All I wanted now was to lie with my feet

up on a bed, in the company of a book.
And my barrel in the corner
—where I'd paid some boys to bring it on a handcart.

One night when I couldn't sleep, I rolled my barrel to my bedside,
and laying my cheek against its staves,
tried to feel what I felt inside it on a late October day.
And though I knew I could never return to that moment
—*there*—with my face against the wood,
I began to rise on its old buoyancy:
And I saw the sky above me, filled with bright autumnal sun.
And the river, white with spray.
And the sweaty back of the boy who'd rowed
—And this time when he cut the rope,
I heard him wish me well.

And I saw the way I tossed across the rapids—
and how I hurtled down the Falls—
and the way I found myself there
—where it seemed there was no one else.
I saw—*I actually saw it!*—how I whirled inside the void
—where my fingers touched my head to let me know *I was alive!*
But this time in the darkness, I heard a whirling sound—
I turned around, and now I saw—
the world was out there too
—Though I knew it couldn't stop to say my name—
as I lay in a dark hotel room, my cheek against its grain.

LAST DAYS [VI-8]

My last few years, on dry weather days,
I'd sit outside the International Hotel on Falls Street.
I could barely see at all—just a glimpse now and then—
as if through a keyhole.
But I had a cane
and knew my way by touch.
I'd bring a pillow from my bed
and set it on the steps,
so I could sit (close to the railing)
—and spread a handful of my postcards
beside my metal cup.

Sometimes a hackman would point me out.
And then a gentleman or lady
—(I couldn't tell until I heard the voice)—
might pass a coin to the driver for a card.
Sometimes with a bit of prompting,
a child's voice might call *hello.*
And occasionally, someone leaned in my direction
and posed a serious question
—but before I could frame a serious reply,
the reins would snap,
and the voices roll away.

Sometimes someone passing
would drop a nickel in my cup
—thinking me a beggar—or at best an old peddler
with some faded cards to sell
—not imagining I had anything to tell—
seeing me crumpled on the steps, so spattered and so small.
Yet inside I still felt vast as the Niagara—
though we both were tired now

and didn't bother to get riled
when they ignored us or abused us
or took us for something else.

I had lost my barrel in an alley one night
—when strange wild winds
came ripping through the Falls
and blew apart my booth.
Perhaps my banner struck me
(at least that's what they told me
when I started to describe what I had seen).
I never saw my barrel after that
—Though at first, I searched for it daily.
But in the end, all the alleys looked alike.
And all the barrels were filled with rain.

I've wondered—was it true—as *someone* told me—
that I didn't need a prop to tell my story.
But I never put his theory to the test.
After that, I kept my history to myself
—as well as that message
that I'd dragged from place to place
for twenty years—at such expense:
I used to tell them, *I am alive*—
I had thought that was a gift,
but now it seemed too thin and tattered
to be of use to anyone.

I guess they'll tell you
how they brought me to the poorhouse
—as if they should be praised.
And they'll say I "came to nothing"

—as if I ought to be ashamed.
And they'll mention I was sick
and eighty-three and blind
—and "should have known better"—
when I sat out on a curb, selling postcards in the sun
to keep myself alive.
But I ask you: *What else should I have done?*

LOOKING FOR THE PARADE

(1999)

HER HEAD

Near Ekuvukeni
in Natal, South Africa,
a woman carries water on her head.
After a year of drought,
when one child in three is at risk of death,
she returns from a distant well,
carrying water on her head.

The pumpkins are gone,
the tomatoes withered,
yet the woman carries water on her head.
The cattle kraals are empty,
the goats gaunt—
no milk now for children,
but *she* is carrying water on her head.

The engineers have reversed the river:
those with power can keep their power,
but *one* woman is carrying water on her head.
In the homelands, where the dusty crowds
watch the empty roads for water trucks,
one woman trusts herself with treasure,
and carries the water on her head.

The sun does not dissuade her,
not the dried earth that blows against her,
as she carries the water on her head.
In a huge and dirty pail,
with an idle handle,
resting on a narrow can,
this *woman* is carrying water on her head.

This woman, who girds her neck
with safety pins, this one
who carries water on her head,
trusts her *own* head to bring to her people
what they need now
between life and death:
She is carrying them water on her head.

TAKING THE COUNT

1

Tonight a soldier is taking photos
on the highway north of Al Jahrah, Kuwait.
He will pass them around when he's back home,
will show his wife
—though maybe not his children—
but certainly the men who teach with him at school,
and later some of the neighbors
—maybe when it's summer
and they're sitting around the pool,
so they can see
how many arms and legs
are sticking out,
and can imagine how many there were,
and a thousand tons of fire pounding down
—and the way the earth shook.

2

Tonight a student is standing in the lights of a patrol car
at the University of Rochester.
He has a can of paint
and has left ten thousand small white marks
on the steps of the university library
—not knowing yet (as no one does)
that there are a hundred thousand—
maybe a hundred and fifty thousand—
to the count.
He is being read his rights,
he is being patted down for weapons,

he is being shoved into the back seat of the car
to be driven to the station—
to be charged "with a defacement
that will take forever to erase."

3

Tonight a priest is picking his way across the sand
that flanks the road to As Salman, Iraq.
He is stopping here and there—
and, one by one,
scratches out a work of mercy.
The shovel in his hands
might have spread manure
on the charred fields
beyond their burned villages,
or might have helped them probe for water
in this winter drought,
but tonight, though uncertain of their rituals,
he is building little mounds
—since there's no way left but this one
to be merciful.

SONNY'S HANDS

for Sonny Ovitt, Yaddo

Sonny told me he "gave up on intelligence long ago,"
It was, he said, "in everyone's best interests."
"Intelligence," he said,
and I let him get away with it.
—Though the whole time he was speaking,
I was thinking
how expert Sonny is at contemplation,
and I was admiring
how he'd designed
the new, sliding shed
for the pool pump
—a feat of instinctive engineering,
acquired from years of noticing
the way things get abused.

But now I *refuse* to agree with him.
—and I refuse to agree with whomever it might be—
whose interests lie
in hiding Sonny's intelligence from him.
"Intelligence," he said.
And I said nothing
(though I know the etymology means:
"the ability to choose between").
Sonny told me he "gave up" on intelligence
and "chose" his hands.
—And God knows where they've been since then:
clearing woods, pulling stumps, and hauling out rocks,
and (most of all) down in foul septic holes
—then driving off in what he calls "the honey wagon."

And here at Yaddo,
I've seen their more delicate workings—
all the welded pedestals and stretched canvases
—and in the woods, the gates of willow they helped set:
I remember the day I came upon them,
and (following their "directions"),
how I found myself in a chamber in the ground
—and knew it was the *universal* womb.
But I didn't know yet
—that when an artist made that place—
so beautiful and terrible
with the raw earth of its walls—
it was Sonny who lifted up the earth
—by each small shovel load.

Sonny says the earth speaks to him—
a call and response—
as he tamps it with the back hoe
that they got here last summer.
Sometimes it tells him to go slowly—
and then discloses what it's hidden:
a pipe or cistern, a trove of old bottles
—or some other treasure he'll uncover
when he shuts off the machine
and gets the short-handled shovel.
"I could write your name
in the earth with that back hoe,"
he once told me—
"but I still like the feel of a tool."

It was a short-handled shovel he used
that spring, "when the ground finally thawed,"
and his "stillborn"
(as he called his child,
who'd been kept all winter in their barn)
"could finally be laid where it belonged."
He told me how he felt—
digging the earth, "so full of life—
even in that tiny hole."
And how, when he struck the rock,
he realized "that no one—
and especially not a child—
should lie forever
with such a huge, hard, lifeless thing."

He described then how he got his truck,
backed it up to the rim,
set the chains to the axle
—and gunned it till he had it out.
But turning back to the neatly tapered mound,
he could see "a hundred smaller stones"
—poking out their fists among the grains.
And though his family was already on their way,
he knelt and raked his bare hands
through that mound—
till he'd sifted out each stone, each pebble,
and scooped them all onto his plaid jacket,
and dumped them with their awful clattering
into the empty, metal bed of his truck.

But Sonny's hands didn't rest—
not even as the mourners came toward him,
bringing that thing so delicate.
He could see what would happen
—with the cardboard wrapping,
damp from the winter in the barn.
And not thinking at all—
about what *anyone* would say—
his hands
scooped up his child from the grass—
and shielding it from all their eyes
against his soiled chest,
he brought it to the earth
—and wrapped it in the blanket he had made.

PLAY-BY-PLAY

Would it surprise the young men
playing softball on the hill to hear the women
on the terrace admiring their bodies:
The slim waist of the pitcher. The strength
of the runner's legs. The torso of the catcher
—rising off his knees to toss the ball back to the mound?
Would it embarrass them
to hear two women, sitting together after dinner,
praising even their futile motions:
The flex of a batter's hips
before his missed swing. The wide-spread stride
of a man picked off his base. The intensity
on the new man's face
—as he waits on deck and fans the air?

Would it annoy them—the way some women
take offense when men caress them with their eyes?
And why should it surprise me that these women,
well past sixty, haven't put aside desire
but sit at ease and in pleasure,
watching the young men move above the rose garden—
where the marble Naiads
pose and yawn in their fountain?
Who better than these women (with their sweaters
draped across their shoulders, their perspectives
honed from years of lovers) to recognize
the beauty that would otherwise
go unnoticed on this hill?
And will it compromise their pleasure,
if I sit down at their table: to listen to the play-by-play
and see it through their eyes?

Would it distract the young men—if they realized
that *three* women laughing softly on the terrace
above closed books and half-filled wine glasses
are moving beside them on the field?
Would they want to know how they've been
held to the light—till some motion or expression
showed the unsuspected loveliness
in a common shape or face?
Wouldn't they have liked to see
how they looked down there—
as they stood for a moment at the plate—
bathed in the light of perfect expectation
—before their shadows lengthened. Before they
walked together up the darkened hill—
so beautiful they would not have
recognized themselves.

POSSESSION

MacDowell Colony

A deer!—nibbling on the few green things
that grow in my strawy meadow.
Mine, we say here: *my* studio, *my* meadow, *my* road.
It is as it is. We were born
to possess it all and more. There's no longer
a chance to change direction. So have one. *Have* a meadow.
Try it on—there are black-eyed Susans in your hair.
Have a deer. Have a deer fly—(I had *two*
of them yesterday. My stained tablet backs me up).
Have a swallow. Try to hold it in your throat
as it goes down beyond the pines of your forest.
But first feel its presence, try to catch
its essence. Before the words intrude.

Or were they there before you even *saw* it?
My. Mine. The exultant mind!—
as incapable as an ant of evading the trail
to its hole. But look down into that hole:
it's full of everything you've seen or can hope to see.
Do you think you could, for once,
see something—maybe a deer—and not *think* the word?
Even if you tried with all your "faculties,"
even if you tricked yourself that you had,
some part of your mind would have whispered *deer*
(the mind's equivalent of saying *mine*).

Now you *possess* it. It is *your* deer.
See how nicely it fits with all the other things:
it finds the stall of its category—the strawy room
in your father's house that was prepared for it.

Wasn't that you at the door with your mother
as she pointed to the things: *meadow, swallow, deer,*
so you would know them when you woke?
The things she overlooked, you discovered
in your books. You showed them to your mind,
and now when you see something rise from the meadow
with its gold furred shape tapering into a sting,
your mind rushes in, pointing to the page:
Honeybee, it tells you. (*My* honeybee.)

Why would you want to stop it now? Didn't you
reward it with gold stars till now it struts like a priest,
mediating all your experience through its psalter?
What are *you*? you ask it.
It sifts the gilt-edged pages of itself, it moves
the satin ribbon to a field of gray—densely coiled
—through which hum the resplendent neurons—
extending themselves, synapse to synapse:
In the pots on their darting hips
is everything you've ever known.
I am your *mind,* it says. *My* mind, it says,
as it contemplates itself—as if it had
created itself—with vanity and humility.

THE BLACK DOG: ON BEING A POET

So that coming to the low wall near the foreman's house
(where a mare is nosing a stallion's heels), I might turn
and see a black dog walking up the hill—
-ashamed that he was dozing and missed a scent,
and now it's filtered in and stirred him, and he must again
make that long, slow climb on stiff, unready joints,
pausing now and then to bark his warning,
yet all the time, his wagging tail.
Till I stand face to face with him:
the pair of us, wondering what he'll do.
He sniffs me liberally, then snorts
and shoves his head into the space he knows
must be beneath my hand—where it fits exactly—
and lets me feel the old, intelligent skull.

And I think how long his journey's been
—how long that head evolved so that it fits my hand—
while keeping all the scents of the world in order.
And how long my hand has been readying itself
to articulate around the sense of him.
And how easily that unsuspected part
(once called the soul or heart)
can pass unnoticed through its unpatrolled borders
and trespass over into his.
So that even after Sartre—(*Even*
after Skinner)—we both can act with purpose and volition
as I stroke, with his ingenuous permission, the black dog's head.
—Not to "tame" him—Not to "elevate" him—
or to use him only as a prop for my cleverness
—*Not even to "contain" him for a moment*—
but to let him move as he pleases—
even if it's back down the hill where he came from—

To move *with* him as he moves. To *move*
as he does. Till a door closes. Or opens.

WHAT TO DO WITH AN INCHWORM

There—on the blackness of my sock,
an inchworm's come to rest,
having dropped from something
while I was walking in the woods.
And it hasn't the slightest sense of danger,
rolled in an "o" in a tuft of weave,
and all the options mine.
Easiest, of course, is pick it off—and step on it
—a swift deliverance to the place it will come to sooner or later,
even if it inches another fifty miles.
(God knows there was a time I would have been relieved
if something had done the same for me.)
But what does an inchworm think about relief?
What does it think at all—
being the center of so much attention?
Nothing. It is asleep
—missing its single intersection with a *higher consciousness.*
It gives no sign of noticing. It hears no
dark thrumming mantra like I heard that winter
when I had no hope of wings.

I've seen a picture in a book:
an inchworm painted near the thing it might become—
a creature of autonomy, capable of flight.
But now *its* life is *mine*
—(my shoe is where it dropped,
not far from the trespassed sock).
But I am a gentler god than the ones I know.
I rouse it with a finger.
It lifts its back—or whatever of itself
agrees to be a back. It becomes an inverted "u."
Oh—you, it has said, and I see it is alarmed—

(just as Adam was when he heard the clock
and knew he was not alone).
I slide a piece of paper underneath it,
and it flails its blind, limbless self over the edge
—probing illimitable space (which begins here and everywhere)
for some nest it thought it owned.
And now something roused in it says,
this is it. Something says, *this is not your place.*
Something says, *there is no place else.*

And so it *allows* me
—(though it can't conceive of me)—
it allows the inconceivable boundaries of my paper
as the only way to negotiate those boundaries.
Look how still it has become—
still and tense as we go through the heavy door—
still and tense across the porch
—and through the lighter door that slams behind us.
If I dropped it now, a bird might find it.
But it has no fear of birds—No equipment for specificity
—just the stark, original fear—without its feathered gown.
I watch how it survives the crisis of its life—
with nothing to measure—nothing to choose. It knows only
hold on. And it holds—as I nudge it against a maple.
It remembers *hold on* as I brush it against an oak.
It holds and it holds-—till I scrape it against a leaf—
a bitten leaf on some kind of sapling I don't know.
And now it goes—lifting itself and flattening itself—
to find what it needs—or at least be free
from the duress of intentions.

BREATH

He's rolled again onto his cracked rib—
and moaning in his sleep until the pressure's
off the fracture—reaches till his fingers
touch my back, and leaning his chest there,
brings his knees under my own.
But who could say this is a burden?
Or that I'm even holding him,
when his arm has come around me
and his face is in my hair,
and whether it's pain
or pleasure brought him here—
where he stirs beneath me now
and sends his breath across my neck?

Who could count the times I've slept
with him—and waking in the night
have found us face to face like God and Adam?
And in the morning on the window,
a single veil of vapor—so I can no longer tell
whose breath is whose.
It would be terror, finding myself so,
but years ago, he left me
in a one-man boat
to paddle out on Mendon Pond
—where dragonflies were mating as they flew.
And drifting on an unknown depth,
and not a soul in sight, I put aside
my terror in that boat filled with his breath
as I understood the way he held me.

There are some who understand displacement—
the ratio of weight to water

—and in the morning in their classrooms,
small children will demonstrate the principles
by dropping half-filled jars in tanks
to show what sinks, what floats.
But in that boat I learned no laws of matter
but saw instead—how with instinct or some grace—
we might find the thing to hold us unrestrained
—and buoy us where we choose to go.
I floated there—joined to his breath—
and let the water take me
for something lighter than I am.
I felt his lightness move beneath me then—
and as he leans his weight
—I feel that lightness now.

from AUTUMN IN EDEN

II

Look how the sun has slipped behind us
—and how everything is suddenly in focus.
Don't those trees reflected on the water
seem as real now as the ones on shore above them
—as if they've always been there—
inverted and supporting all that weight?
But it's only a trick of the light—
(no other creature would even notice them).
And all that red and gold that we stand admiring—
letting ourselves be moved by it
(as if it were intentional and meant for us)
—it's only some chemical breaking down
that makes them
look beautiful when dying—
the way nothing else does.
If we were trees, we'd see it as an abomination
—and try to hide ourselves.

You're asking *me* their names?
—you *know* I'm bad with trees!
But this one's growing fishing bobs,
and—look here—a rubber glove.
You're right, it probably came here with a fisherman
—maybe one who couldn't stand the touch of worms.
But to me, the fish are worse
—with their scales all sharp and slippery,
and all that accusation in their small, flat eyes
when you realize you could put them back,
and how badly they want it—and you don't.
Last week I saw a boy on the dock by Van's trailer,

pulling up sunnies, one after another,
holding each by its tail,
"I name you Charlie," or "I name you Paul"
—then slamming its head against the boards.
He made me think of God.

I think there's too much in the water
—I can't look at it the way I used to.
No, it's not those cups I mean—(though they'll probably
outfloat ten generations of our children)
—It's more than the debris: *Once, I could see*
my face. Now, in every drop, I'm forced to see
a thousand things I know from books,
swimming by with all their Latin names—
enlarged so that they're bigger than my face.
If we were meant to know them, wouldn't our eyes
be completely different?
Yes, it's what we said we wanted:
the *knowledge* of everything
—all that beautiful science—
And mortality, pushed off into some corner
—so you don't believe it's there
until you feel it through your shoes.

But the old idea of living forever,
where you could run into each other now and then
—it's gone—just like that!
I used to believe in eternity—*I still do*
—I just don't think it's got anything to do with us.
It's the same way with the sun:
I used to believe it rose and set, and I can't quite stop
—even though I know it hasn't happened

for four hundred years.
Wait just a second—
if we turn up here, we can walk for a while
on the tracks (it should be drier there).
But we'll have to pick some marker
—to find our way back later.
The tree with the crow? Don't always joke.
It will be darker then, and if we lose our way,
you'll be the first to blame me.

THE GOOD "BAD KIDS"

The good "bad kids" are racing through the water,
over the slippery rocks, among the jets of spray—
barefoot, bare to the waist—
with their black jeans rolled up to their knees,
and their long lank hair dripping down their backs—
and the sunlight
nuzzling every part of them it can.

And you know their mothers would kill them
if they saw them here
—where they could slip away forever
among these boulders.
And you know that by stopping here,
you're giving them
encouragement.

Look how they're trying to impress you—
growing more and more reckless—
as they scramble up onto the highest boulders,
whooping and waving—
though you're old enough to be their mother
—but you're far enough away
so they can't tell.

So you head to the town at the bottom of the hill—
though you hear them calling for you to come back
—to see something so daring
it could make your mouth water for a taste of it.
But you're already gone—
you've gone miles beyond their careless summer
—and you've seen too many good things fall.

In the town you pay your bills.
Pick up a paper. And the books you'd ordered.
When you make your way back up the hill,
the day has cooled,
the sun has slipped behind some trees.
And the only sound's
the rushing of the falls.

The good "bad kids" are lying in some field,
wringing out the water from their hair,
rolling down
the soaked legs of their jeans,
making up some lies—
rehearsing their whole lives
—getting ready to go home.

PETERBOROUGH PET STORE

for Lucy Grealey

"Iguanas: $22.50
(one with the broken tail: 19.00)."
Guinea pigs, a sign says, cost "11.00"
(but the cage below
has a pair of long-eared rabbits,
who'd trip over themselves if they could go anywhere).
The owner is congenial
—much more so than
the unshaven, white-haired man in
the stretched white tee shirt,
who's hobbled in on his crutches "to watch."
We've come to see parrots. But there are no parrots.
The prankish Lord of Chance has led us here—
just in time (10 A.M. on a Tuesday)
—to see a rat and boa dance.

We've missed the first part
—the fast, beginning moves
in the small, rectangular tank on the bottom shelf.
Now the rat (which looks singularly appealing
in a Beatrix Potter sort of way)
is, as the ballroom crowd might say,
"putting her whole self into it—giving it *everything* she's got."
She's flipping her tail, she's kicking her dainty feet up in the air—
she's twitching her head from side to side
—and clearly *no* means *no* to her.
"Do you mind?" Lucy asks me,
"I've never seen this."
(Either have I.)

"Would you like to buy it?" the owner asks.
"The furry one," I reply.

He laughs and tries to deflect us (perhaps still hoping for a sale):
"It's the first time I've seen that tarantula
climb up the side of his tank."
But I can't be seduced away by anything peripheral.
In *this* tank is *death.*
And I mean to *learn* it
—and every move it makes.
Look at its competent embrace—
There's not the slightest straining
in the long single muscle
of itself. It moves gently
through its own impeccable curve. It takes *its time.*
Even after the rat has stopped fumbling for alternatives
—when it's left with only its durable staring—
during which, the moment—as elusive as the *arrival* of the soul—
passes unnoticed right in front of our eyes:
the rat is dead.

I have no interest in seeing it devoured.
This is dinner. Like every night
—when we choose not to fathom how the cow bellowed
till its cleft head
fell into the steaming pile
of its own shit.
We can't even *imagine* it.
Just last week in a museum, I heard twenty children,
unprompted—cry in unison, *eeeyooo!*
when a lecturer told them that the tyrannosaurus
ate things already dead

—what the hell do they think *they're* doing
when they stop in the cafeteria?

Oh, but we do it *so much more decorously* than this boa.
We take the high road—
like that scientist, who, in a fabulously expensive white suit,
went up in the shuttle a month ago,
and with a guillotine (a small, precise *guillotine!*
engineered especially for him),
decapitated twenty rats—
and not for anyone to eat
—but simply for the sake of *knowledge*.
And now I'm kneeling at that same feast—
while the boa is conducting my experiment,
and the rat is performing my lab duty.
"Let's go," Lucy says, as one head
swallows another. (It's not that she's disgusted.
It's just taking too long—and we're on our way
to get some coffee in the bookshop.)

Before we go, I ask the owner
where the rats come from—
does he buy them from someone—
or raise them somewhere for prey?
(I want to fathom the full possibility of my horror
—only later do I consider the cows of the abbatoir.)
Know then—as I now do—
that in the Peterborough Pet Store,
there is a room with a closed door. (It is on the left,
should you wish to find it.) And it is full
of mice and rats—grey, brown and albino.
Some are standing with their two yellow teeth

pressed against the glass. Some are not yet weaned.
One lives alone with his treadwheel.
And there is food—enough to last their lifetimes—

in bulging bags that say: *I-ams-I-ams-I-ams.*
"We sell them as pets—if anybody wants them,"
says the owner. "And when the boa starts moving,
I just come in and pick one."

I remember when Sheila (she had just turned twenty)
said, "I'm not afraid of being dead.
You're *nothing* then,
and you've got *nothing* to worry about.
But dying—I'm not sure what that's going to be like."
A few days later,
she just sat up and stared.
I don't ask Lucy what it was like
when that *same thing*
coiled around her
and got part of her face.
She was only nine then,
and it's hard to fathom how she was able to escape
—when it seemed so sure of itself, so practiced.
We sip our coffee.
Already I sense it slipping away—
going off to digest what it's already grasped.
We've moved on to other things.
Lucy tells me she has a parrot named Oliver.
He's just beginning to speak.

from 20TH CENTURY CREATIVITY

1

The prisoner in the Stalag
remembers the opening of a poem.
He taps it on the pipes in code.
The others listen in their walls
like lonely new recruits—
glad to read anybody's mail.
Next week another man
thinks of the next line.
Now they wait like tunnelers,
tense in the middle of a dark airless hole,
afraid they won't
get to the end of it.

2

The prisoner in the Gulag
spots the bits of dust in a corner of his cell.
When the glare from the guard is gone,
he sculpts them with his nail—
kings and queens and pawns—
the size of beans and rice.
Even though there is no light,
his fingers know them.
When they are noticed,
they are crushed and swept away.
He begins again. And again.
His opponent waits patiently.

3

The prisoner marching from Bataan
remembers the lilacs
outside his home—the smell of his mother's
Sunday roast—the scent
of his sweetheart's hair
—as she pressed her lips on his
the night before he left.
He lays his face down in the ditch
—only his mouth and nose
because there wasn't very much
in anyone's bowels this morning
—but there's enough to end it.

4

The prisoner in Treblinka
strips beside her daughter.
She is startled to see the budded
breasts above the pleated ribs.
She glances at the others—
the slackened flesh
of half-dead women
—flesh, like her own.
One of them is looking at her daughter:
"A girl who'd be a bride," the look says.
She whispers to her daughter,
"The shower will be warm."

from LOOKING FOR THE PARADE

for Tony Phillips, Memorial Day

I

The women from Yaddo's kitchen
told us there'd be a parade.
Ever since they were children (Long before
their parents were children!) there had been
a parade. We didn't ask where it would go,
knowing it would have to go down
whichever street lies along the backbone of the town
—and here in Saratoga is called Broadway.
And it would march from wherever the gentry live
to whatever park holds the cannon,
scrapped from whichever war
— like this one on Union Avenue,
where this morning, spike-haired punks are sleeping,
and a bride is yawning, and a pair of twins,
one blue-, the other, brown-eyed,
are improvising a ceremony at the side of their stroller.

And we were certain the whole town
would be waiting on this grass
where the tamed mallards poke for crumbs—
and a pair of grey-haired lovers touch
with such slow tenderness—that we smile at their progress
—till they suddenly grow self-conscious.
And at that moment, a whistle in the distance
would dispatch a coterie of drums and brass
from a boys' club. Then, a drill team,
fitted out with decoy guns and banners.
A squad of twirlers and cadets.
A company, fatigued and slightly out of breath

from Vietnam. A women's auxiliary,
uniformly overweight, but stepping lightly.
—And bringing up the rear, a white-haired man,
pushed by (one last time) in his rolling silver chair.

And we would stand among the people of this town,
waiting for that parade to come
—our heads inclined in the same direction—
to catch the first uncertain notes
or glimpse a flash of colors
between the bobbing heads and shoulders,
that line their route down Broadway.
And despite our belief that we could keep our distance,
some clumsy salute or off-key rallying strain
might touch us as we listen—
might quicken our pulses as we wait in formation,
pressed shoulder to shoulder.
Then we'd have to struggle for a moment,
blink our eyes, force ourselves to smile,
and whisper to each other how corny it all is
—with wave after wave of passing American life.

II

Still looking for the parade, we drive up Broadway—
hearing, blow by blow, what will happen
When Johnny Comes Marching Home on the FM radio.
The melody is gloomy—despite the lyric's try
for a jaunty encouragement.
They must have know, even then, in our internecine war—
after the unfulfilled waiting, the contradictory news
and the unexplained silence
that permits a general, willful delusion,
that there might be no parade.
Even today, there are no *men cheering,*
no *boys shouting.*
The ladies—they have not *turned out*
—not even the women from the kitchen.
There's still no sign of a parade.
Though we've kept on looking for what seems a century.

I point with hope to a corner
where a man with a rolling cart—
hung with T-shirts and Caribbean art—
is arranging his display as if preparing for a crowd
—(But Tony's sure there was a cart there all last week).
We spot a family turning onto Broadway
with caps and visors, binoculars and cameras.
But they're too well-dressed—
they've got no folding chairs or cooler chests
—(Only tourists from another city).
And what of those three girls on that bench,
tanned and leggy and a little giggly?
They scan us as we pass—then go back to eating lunch,

without a sign of disillusionment
—(knowing that in time,
someone better will come by and pick them up).

But then at a light—a man in a tie-dyed shirt,
middle-aged and thick in the waist,
calls to us from the curb, "What time is the parade?"
He's been looking up Broadway,
he's been waiting for Johnny.
He wants to give him that *hearty welcome*—
—It's a new age now—we all want to *feel gay.*
We've put aside our revolutions—our radical opinions
—Even our campus insurrections are fading into history.
It's time to walk with Johnny to the park
and stand beside him (through the long-
winded speeches, filled with peaceful lies).
It's time to shake his hand—
and go and spread the news: that Johnny's
come marching home—and his legs still work
—and maybe all of that was worth it.

V

Relaxed on our graves,
we raise the tagged lids of our lunch pails,
and, noticing our names, we joke about how well
they make us fit among our company.
Only two cars pass us in an hour,
and then there's a rumbling down below
—and up between the markers, rolls a pack of bikers,
(ignoring all the set-in-stone requests for "rest" and "peace").
There are ten—with a grizzly bearded leader at the head—
fitted out in all his militant regalia:
the red and blue tattoos, the gleaming metal-studded cuffs
—and the vest that only skims his fleshy torso.
He stops his bike twenty feet from us
and stares our way, considering his plans.
The rest fan out behind him—
fidgety—in the sun, their chains and leather.

Their motors turning over,
two forward ones begin a drill maneuver:
making narrow turns
on the graves that say "Infant" and "Mother."
Though we can't begin to comprehend its meaning—
or predict where their pageantry is leading—
it's clear who's signaling the moves (he grimaces occasionally,
so I can see that most of his lower teeth are gone).
When at last he's ready, he raises his right hand,
and his right-hand man pulls up till he's nearly at our feet,
and without dismounting or shutting off his engine,
he leans and asks: "Where's the parade?"
As they rumble back down, with undaunted bluster,

we smile at each other—
glad to be left with the safe, quiet dead
in the clouds of settling dust.

But we've got no plans to stay with them *forever*—
pressed shoulder to shoulder in their regimented rows—
in the kind of place our new age doesn't bother with at all.
But the grass still grows here,
and someone comes and mows—and leaves a whistle in the air
to move among the immovable formation:
the long parade going nowhere.
No, you'll never find us here!
—We might be scattered in a stream—or under a favorite tree—
fooling ourselves
that we've escaped the *ultimate* conformity.
But despite our hopes to avoid its trappings,
or at least be able to explain
that *we* were different—that we liked to joke—and never
took things too seriously, we'll take our places, just as they did
—and find it just as easy.

DANCING ON THE EDGE

(2002)

THE FENCE

A family says goodbye to a boy soon to be deported to a death camp.
(*New York Times* travel section photo caption)

It's chicken wire—the kind you see everywhere—and it probably
is tall. Although, with the top cropped off, it's hard to tell.
The only pole visible was, till recently, a sapling tree—
it's gangly—and still a little knobby—as if someone didn't try
or couldn't spare the time to do it right. Besides,
there are no chickens on either side.

It appears we're on the *inside*—behind the boy, sitting cross-legged
with his elbows on his knees. His pants are short, and the pale
flesh of his thigh (seen here in black and white) is as bright
as the six-point star on his shoulder blade. Though we can't guess
the expression on his face, he looks relaxed
as he sits and waits between two clumps of weeds.

The ones on the *outside* are easier to see: the two who might be
his sisters—girls with thick black hair, each resting on an elbow
with her legs stretched on the ground. The one on the left
looks away into the distance; the other, closer,
with her cheek pressed on her shoulder, looks down
where nothing is—and meets its gaze.

The fourth—a little younger than the rest—sits slumped against
the pole and hunches over. With the same short hair and identical cap,
he's staring past the mirror that's his brother. His sober
eyes hang on the fence that stands in his line of sight,
saying, *narrow your shoulders, try to hide,*
but in just a little time, you'll *be inside.*

The fifth, at the right—clearly older than the others—
kneels low and feels the fence against her face. Though she looks serene
as she whispers her goodbyes, her hands betray her—
she must be his mother—wringing her yet wet fingers in the
apron she'd have hung up in the kitchen
if the boxcars weren't filling at the siding.

She has so much to tell him, and the fence is so obliging,
though it's full of air—hardly even there—it's arms keep intertwining—
making diamond shapes around their eyes like a secret leaded window,
and she's reminding him through the panes to say his prayers,
to answer promptly whatever he's asked, and pass
a message to his father, who's gone ahead.

Oh yes, he'll remember, he'll remember the fence
and everything she said—he'll remember all his life.

ETERNITY

Because Lena's not yet three,
she doesn't know the reason for this place.
"I like *this* little house. And *this* little house,"
she says as she loops around them
—the play-size "houses" of the dead.
Here in Key West, as in New Orleans,
where the land and sea are nearly level,
some are set just above the surface,
and Lena leans on their "big stone beds."

But since Lena's not yet three,
she doesn't know what any of it means:
She doesn't know where the earth rolls away to
every night while she's asleep—
or who rolls with it—some above it, some below.
And because she doesn't know,
she moves in waves of joy
like the spirit on the surface of the waters
—before it ever thought of light.

She squeezes between two "beds"
that are stretched out side by side—
one's bigger than the other—
and pats them, left then right,
and reunites what slipped apart a hundred years ago:
a mother—and her child of a day.
We learn this from their surnames and the dates
—but Lena doesn't read,
and there's no reason to explain.

We watch her bolt through the gate
where the men of the *Maine*

sail on in shipshape rows
as she splashes among their stones.
"God Was Good to Me," one epitaph proclaims,
but Lena has no knowledge of God.
Or his goodness. Or the opposite implied
by what's said on every side
in the silent houses of the dead.

When we say it's time to go, she runs ahead again,
drops down before an upright stone,
and moves her finger across its surface.
She runs to another, repeats her motions—
as she read its lines out loud:
The name. The date. And the other.
—And though she's still too young to read,
she reads them anyhow:
"I love you. I love you. I love you."

—But how could she know?—How could she know
what would trump all the mansions of gold?

NOW WE KNOW

We've been wondering what that duck's
been doing by the pond all month—
ambling by our apartment windows
in her quirky isolation—even though it's nearly
winter, and she must have known
the snow was coming and the other ducks had gone.
I'd guessed she must be defective—
it could happen in a million different ways:
just one snag in one strand of DNA
and she could be missing
whichever part of whichever lobe
says to a duck: *Get going.*

Last month, when ice was forming near
the shore, I'd sometimes see her in the center
—where our stolen pumpkin was still floating,
but now it's December,
and it's anchored to the surface,
where it blazes like something meant to warn us.
And there's that duck parading on the ice,
and three boys (two with bikes)
throwing stones in her direction.
She walks around them casually—
which makes me think she probably can't fly.
In any case, I've got to save her from those boys.

I grab my coat. And a loaf of whole wheat bread.
I'll try to coax them to feed her. Instead of
kill her. But the boys reject my offer.
They say they'd rather throw their stones:
We're not hurting anyone. And to prove it,
the biggest boy hurls one down—the size of

a football—it doesn't go through
but makes a huge concussion—
still, the duck doesn't move.
But from the reeds—just below where they've been standing,
a duckling skitters across the ice
to the reeds on the opposite side.

So now we know what she's been up to.
And what's gone wrong here.
And at once, something comes upon the boys—
now they *want* to feed her. But the small nervous one
(the one without a bike) grabs the bag from
my hand and runs around the pond,
trying to find the duckling. But he can't.
When he scuffles back, dragging the bag of bread,
the three of them go at it—tearing it up
till they've torn the whole loaf, and she's asking
for more, and the boys are asking me what to do.
I tell them, *I don't know. It's late, it's cold—I'm going in.*

As I sip my coffee at the window, I watch the boys
arguing about the duck. Their voices drift up—
getting mixed up with the news on my radio.
It's all about a NASA crew who'll fix the Hubble telescope
so the universe will look as clear as we'd like it to.
They've been planning their mission for a year—
they've got a hundred and fifty tools—
two of everything they'll need. And if they succeed,
we'll know how old the universe is,
and how our galaxy began. And we'll understand
the nature of black holes. And someone's
bound to tell us what to do.

For now, the boys keep trying their old maneuvers:
counting to three, then lobbing their stones—
they're trying to break the ice—*for her*—
while she stands on shore beside them,
looking as if she's hired them. I'm sure they're the ones
who stole our pumpkin for the fun of it,
but now the fun's gone out of them—
now they know they guilty secret of the universe—
right outside their apartment windows.
They don't even cheer when a stone goes through.
Though they've got a hole, it's much too small
for a duck to float around in—and they know.

I watch the biggest boy crawl down beside the hole,
and pound his heels against its sides to make it wider.)
When he can't stand the icy water any longer,
he pulls off his shoes and socks and
pedals home—where someone's bound to yell at him.
Now the middle one takes his turn—
easing his bike down the steep incline.
But the weight of the bike and the gravity of the world
want to drag him into the hole. He strains his whole
small self against them, inching his way—
till he can *thump* its front wheel on the ice. But it bounces up—
the ice won't break. No matter how many times he tries.

I can see he's in tears as he looks up at my window—
before I start to wave, he shoots me a look of hate.
It's nearly dark, when the small one finally
drops the bag and follows the middle one home.
Yet it's easier to see that duck—now that she's slid
into the hole—where she's floating around

as the boys had wanted her to. I glance around the
surface of the pond, hoping to see her duckling. But I don't.
Should I wish it spring? Or maybe death?
Neither of which will come quick enough.
My empty bag is skittering on the ice—
the wind's inside, telling it what to do.

MASTER OF THE SITUATION

Though your bike's been taken,
you want to get to work, and now your ankle
twists on a stone poking from the dirt
on the road to your studio.
Go with the twist, something tells you.
It's not something *you* would ever know—
but just as drivers guess on icy roads
to go into a skid—not to stop it or correct it—
you let your force go with it. You know you're not
the master of the situation.

No, your force is nothing
to the fulcrum of something's stone—
something that's always dropping
little gauntlets in your path—
like that diminutive red squiggle near your ankle:
a tiny red newt on its great safari
across the wide Serengeti of the road.
It takes its slow winding detours around the stones—
just the way you always drive through little towns
to avoid a shot cut up a mountain.

You squat down to watch it. You can tell
it's aware of you—but because you haven't squashed it,
it ignores you. God, you want to hurry it—
you want to be there with your magnanimous cheers
when it stands with its medal on the top step
of a pedestal, weeping to "The Anthem of Newt Land."
You think about picking up one of those
brown pine needles, that are lying
all over the road—You'd like to show it
who controls the situation.

But you refrain. Because something tells you—
something that's clearly on its side—
as it wades on its piddly feet through the grains of sand
like someone swimming slowly—
just for the pleasure of it.
It pauses by a stone—pauses, pauses, doing nothing—
that's the way you think of it
as it stands there—brighter than anything you can
see in any direction—and wields against you
the mountainous weapon of its patience.

FOR ANONYMOUS

The shy young writer from Natchez covers his mouth when he speaks.
On the night I arrived, when I asked the others sitting with me
to tell me there names, he exclaimed,
"Are we gonna go around the table?"
And the night we all were saying how everyone there
reminded us of someone else we knew,
he dropped his eyes and snapped, "Y'all quit talking about me!"
Before we even got to him.

He's very handsome. Though it hasn't been easy to notice.
We know nothing about him.
Except that he drives a pickup. And once wrote passionate letters
that some foolish woman burned.
(The words slipped out one night when he had a little wine,
and there was no way to retrieve them.)

He always dresses in white. The way some Southerners do.
"He's the ghost of Mark Twain," a playwright once joked.
Though to me he looks more fragile.
A bit like Virginia Woolf.

But he only wears white. Nothing but white—
Like doctors—who like things sterile.
Or a priest in the darkness of a jungle.

Or the ones who keep things quiet in asylums.
Or a bride inviolate for her husband.

Or the angels in the clouds,
or dead men in their shrouds

or others who want to be

invisible.

TOBY'S BODY

for Tobias Schneebaum, Yaddo

We all have seen it.
In the slide show he gives each summer.
There he is! (or *There you are!*) someone will say
—when suddenly, among the Asmat of New Guinea,
a flash of pale male flesh,
wearing Toby's younger face
(and nothing else) appears.
Though he might seem out of place,
he shows no embarrassment—
he's only a rarity—a welcome anomaly
—among a tolerant contingent of the race.

So I'm glad to see *once more*
that he's doing all right there—
looking eager (though egregiously
white) for his rebirth ceremony—
crawling humbly and adroitly
(for a man of twenty-five)
beneath the legs of the whole village!
(It's no surprise that twenty-three tribes
adopted him.)

But it's different at the pool an hour later
(*an hour—and fifty years!*)
—and now the others who've arrived
after watching Toby's slides,
have slipped inside the pool house to strip.
But Toby, thin and a little bent,
still getting over the replacement of his hip,
is pacing the deck
in long black pants.

He glances across the fence to where I'm
standing (on the *outside,* where their van
just dropped me off).
"The lights are much too bright tonight,"
he says, and I agree—
though it's no concern to *me.*
—I say goodnight to Toby
and head back to my room.

Among the Asmat, being naked must be easy—
of course, "we're *all born* naked"
—but the Asmat spend their days
and even *die* so. And at night,
use the skulls of their enemies
for pillows (now *those* are people
with nothing to hide!).

I'm sure by now, the others
have come out to the poolside
—with their bodies tanned and toned
into magnificent disguises.
I wonder if, by now, Toby's
slid out of his clothes,
and slipped into the water beside them.
I wonder if they'll look at him with pleasure—
and soothe the painful ribbon of his scar.
Will they stand and spread their thighs
and invite him under?

WHAT MAKES US HAPPY

I see my neighbor, Gene,
coming home with Gracie in his arms.
On the way home from his hardware store each night,
he takes her for a swim below the bridge.
The first time, she got stranded on some rocks,
and though he tried for half an hour,
there was no way he could reach her.
All he could do was listen to her whine—
till suddenly she stopped—flopped back in. And swam.
She's a retriever—and black like Polly,
who's a little bit of everything—and getting old now.

Last night Gene confided that what makes him happy
is watching dogs swim—*There are different*
things for everyone, he said.
I watch him carry Gracie up the steps
while Polly sits in the truck like a lady.
Polly knows all the old tricks she's supposed to.
But Gracie's new. Gene takes her out each night—
at two—then again at five. He asked me
was I bothered by her noise.
I said I never hear her. (Which isn't true.)

In the fall, the last of Gene's boys
will head off to college. It's hard to let go—
to watch your kids go off to be someone else.
I watch him head back to the pickup—
where Polly's still waiting with his twelve-pack
(he brings one home each night).
Across the lawn on the other side,
our neighbor Jim and his good friend Ethel
sit beneath the silver maple, eating supper.

He looks older—now that Eduardo's left him—
or maybe since this summer he has a grandchild.

Gene's older boys are home for the weekend.
And busy with a basketball (they don't even
look his way as he goes in).
Though he got that brand-new backboard
to lure them back, he and they
don't have as much to say to each other anymore.
Still, they'll keep us up till midnight
with their dribbling—*there are different*
things for everyone. It can be teething
or barking. Growing pains or grieving—

but eventually, our whole street falls asleep,
and in the morning we all rise
and head off in our different directions—
like those people we used to read about in school:
who drove for different distances,
at different speeds, in different lengths of time.
I hope by now they've all arrived
and found the thing that made them go,
or maybe made a turn somewhere
—and were surprised to find something even better.

THE DIVISION OF LABOR

They meet again at the table,
he facing south with a view of the street,
and she to the east where only the tallest trees
have a glint of light now.
They spread their napkins and begin—
as if through the grille in a dark booth in an old church,
and she tells him about some foolish or careless
thing she did that day,
and he must rally himself
from his slow occupation with his plate
to say something about how foolish or careless
she is, or always was,
or has become.

And in house after house as the lights go on,
and the trees roll their spires from the sun,
he turns away from her
and glances at the street where he sees nothing—
though anyone passing might see him so clearly,
and he mentions some foolish or careless
thing he did that day
so she can say, "That wasn't a big thing,"
or, "No one will even remember it tomorrow."
And they keep laboring like that—
laboring together—till they're both satisfied—
and he drops his crumpled napkin
beside her folded one.

BEING LIGHT

You've had that dream again—
the one that shows up now and then,
the way things do when a clue's been overlooked.
What have you missed that you're meant to know?—
that you're a piece of light—
a light glowing in a sphere of other lights—
like the bits of ice that form the rings of Saturn.

Last night you found your place
among a billion others there—
not *in* the sphere, but *being* the sphere—
somewhere beyond your everyday existence.
It's hard to come back from there—
to span that incredible distance—
and have to rebuild your whole frame of consciousness.

It's not like after the typical dream of myriad confusions,
where, at most, you're unsure of *where* you are—
or *who*. But after being light,
you're not even sure *what* you are anymore.
It takes a long time to figure it all out—
and even longer to get your identity up and running
before anybody notices it's gone.

It's not the kind of dream you rush to tell anyone—
not even your husband—sitting across the table
with his coffee and his paper
and the events of the whole world,
which seem so pressing—with their specific names and dates—
obscuring his face
and competing with what you'd really like to say.

So you sit and stir your cup—
waiting for the right moment—when the wings of everything
will be folded up—and it's just the two of you again
in the pure, curious light of Eden.
But when he finally lifts his eyes,
he's already on the stairs, hurrying up to shave—
to get his suit and tie on and drive an hour—

to finish what wasn't finished yesterday
—or begin what he'll have to go back and finish tomorrow.
How can you stop him now, and say,
"We're all pieces of light, glowing somewhere together,
and it's actually kind of nice."
How can you delay him
when he's got so much to hurry to?

THE MINE

for Arne and Julia Bjork

He's in the west part. She's in the east. She's
half paralyzed, she can't speak—
and is apt to have a cry or fit at anything
—and once or twice she's smeared
her feces on the wall. Yet today
I watched her lean forward in her wheelchair
to stroke the hand of a wordless old woman,
who was moaning in the middle of the hall.
She's gotten fast a propelling herself
with her "good food" as he calls it—
she wears a trim white tennis shoe—she's still
slim and beautiful. He's lanky, boyish, blue-eyed.
She waits inside the glass doors till he comes,
and if he's five minutes late, she grab his hand
and shed big wet tears of relief all over it
as he leans to kiss her cheek.

His eyes are going to glaucoma,
and his legs can hardly make it over to her court.
He's eighty-eight, and still talks about
some "radical new surgery" for each of them.
"When the weather gets warmer, I'll take you out
and whirl you around like Fred Astaire."
She smiles to let him know that she's aware of
what he means. I lift my camera. "Fix your hair,"
he tells her, "or you won't look like a Playboy bunny."
She grins uncertainly till the flashbulb goes,
and a nurse with tiny rosebuds on her coat
wheels her off to "solitary" to feed her
(she's too distracted in the common room to eat)—

after, he'll have to reach inside her cheek
to get the food she hasn't swallowed.

"What will she do?" he asks, "when I can't
cross the courtyard anymore?" I hold the door
while he shuffles through slush to my rental car,
and we're off to see the house in Grindstone—
"where she never got to live," he reminds me.
We descend the steep hill through the grim
back-alley streets of trimless boxy houses—
miners' side-by-sides—without a tree in sight
—and the tunneling still rumbling underneath.
She grew up in one of these. But why on God's earth
did she want to come back at eighty-four?
She was packing in the city when the stroke hit her.
On our way out of town, we pass the cemetery.
"That's where I'll be soon," he says. "Aunt Julie too.
The two of us—under the ground together."

THE HUNT

Three fox kits in the twilit field—
the long grass left along the road,
the mist thick by the tree line—
and they are—*(say it!)*—they are *frolicking!*—

even if you're ashamed
of the old unruly word,
even if all the uninhibited play
has drained away from you,

even if the road rushes by
toward the wide houses with the blinded lights
where matrons in the mirrors
are donning tight tan breeches for the ride,

even if the hounds
are crowding at the portals of the kennels,
even if the master
is fastening the strap beneath his chin,

even if the horse hooves come pounding down the field,
where their fathers' fathers' fathers
and their mothers' mothers' mothers
tossed their russet snouts to sniff the wind,

even if they'll cry out, "What are our sins?—
tell us, what are our sins?"
as the pack closes in
with a blood-lust baying for the bite—

tonight they are *frolicking!*—
neither father nor mother in sight—
but the den nearby, and the field wide—
newly mowed for the hounds and riders.

WHERE IT'S TAKING US

At first it seems we're in a car—though it must be
a bus or maybe a ferry or something even bigger
because everyone is here, everyone standing
so close together, everyone laughing so giddily
because there are so many hills to go up and down,
and we're going so fast, and there's nothing to hold on to—
but that thin railing, and so many people
leaning on that rail, so many people pressing toward that rail
that it's impossible for most of us to get anywhere near it.
And you know the way it is—when someone starts laughing,
how everyone joins in: it's completely contagious
and beyond our control and we'd rather laugh than do anything.

And see that woman up there by the rail,
laughing like that baby at the airport, whose father kept lifting her
up to the ceiling, over and over, higher and higher,
and the father laughing, and the baby laughing,
everyone in sight laughing, and no one seeing how close that baby
was getting to the ceiling—and it wasn't my place to intrude.
And there's that woman laughing—like that baby
heading for disaster—laughing with such abandoned laughter
that she's stumbling and staggering and grabbing on to
everyone around her till none of us can stand straight any longer
because we're all in this together, and I've just
bumped that man with the gun in his hand.

It's hardly a gun, of course. Look, he's showing us
where the paint is peeling off. It's a toy gun, of course.
Look how square and crude it is. (Why, I've got a pen
that looks much more sinister.) And besides, isn't everyone
laughing at that gun? Why, that gun can't fool anyone.
And him? Why, he doesn't even know which way

to point it. He's got it by the barrel. He's got it
upside down. And now he's pointing it at himself,
till our sides are splitting because it's so amusing
and it's going so fast like a roller coaster ride or
the starship *Enterprise,* and there's nothing
strapping us in and no one knows who's driving.

And don't we like what he's doing with that gun?
It's the only thing *happening*. (All the rest keeps repeating—
all the rest just is.) Now he' showing us how there are
no bullets in the gun. Spin the chamber around, the whole thing's
full of air! Now he's shooting out the overhead lights.
He's pretending (of course) but I swear I heard
the lights go *ping, ping, ping,* and it's harder to see now,
and we're laughing so much harder—because it's gotten
so much darker, and now everyone has gotten the idea:
everyone's wondering what he's going to shoot next—
because you don't get a gun—you don't take a gun somewhere—
unless you mean to use it. That's the whole point, isn't it?

And now he's pointing it out the window of whatever we're in—
the bus or ferry or the world. And he's pointing it
at that other world of whatever isn't in here with us—
where we're having such a good time, trying to keep
from falling, despite the hills that keep coming up, over and over,
higher and higher, just when we were sure we were past
the worst of them. And wouldn't you say that the man
with the gun is my husband? Or your husband?
Or maybe you? And wouldn't you say that the gun
is my son's old BB pistol that feel out of the box
in the moving van with one green shoe and a tin of jasmine tea
where Chinese boys in pigtails smile so agreeably
as they run in circles with their lanterns?

And can you see how there's a light glowing around that gun?
And *ping, ping, ping,* the windows are all gone.
And it's wildly funny—it's our inside joke—because we know
it isn't loaded. And it's even funnier when we see those little girls—
three identical little girls—standing at the curb
waiting for their bus. And you can see that they're strange
little girls because they're all dressed alike in clothes
that none of us would wear. And it's so funny because
they think that we're their bus. It's so funny that that woman
has collapsed. She's down on her knees, and everyone shouting,
go, go, go, and the gun pointing out the window
or the space where the windows were.

And now the little girls are leaning toward us—
expecting that we're something else, expecting that
we've come to help them get to wherever they have to go.
And isn't that me, trying to say *no*—just a tiny whimper
of a *no*—that no one could possibly make out
above the wild laughter? But now everyone is yelling at me.
Everyone is telling me that *there must be something*
to point at. That if those little girls weren't there,
it would have to be someone else. That if those girls
weren't there, there would be nothing to
point at, nothing to shoot at, nothing to amuse us
as we keep going faster wherever this thing is taking us.

JUMPERS

after Sarah Charlesworth's Stills

I

He's blown-up. So he's life-size.
Yet the L. A. man is going to die.
It's predictable. Unstoppable.
He's diagonal. In a straight line.
He's got his arms wide. Like a spinning game.
With a sixties look. In a plain
white shirt and (rippling) black trousers—
what half the civilized world
wore at the time. He's a no
one. He's an any
one. I know it's going
to be a long way
down.

2

But the man in Ankara, identically dressed,
going headfirst (and so close to the ground it takes my breath)
hangs poised like a rubber stamp that's set to mark him *"canceled"*
when his body scuds through
his skull with a liquid thud.

3

Yet I'm more intrigued by the woman in Madrid,
who drops listlessly with dangling legs,
and doesn't seem distressed
at how the speed of her momentum
has raised a breeze that's forced her skirt
to drift above her waist—
see, it's wrapped around her face
like a hanged man's hood—
and leaves her blinded
to whatever fate awaits her—
whether concrete, hell, or heaven—
she'll face that curtain later.

4

But it's the fourth who beckons me—
look how gracefully she flies—
her arms stretched out before her.
She's young—and dressed like anyone's
daughter might have been during the war.
In the barbershop window below her,
Uncle Sam points sternly to whoever isn't there.
She doesn't care—now that she's sailing
beside the vertical sign of the Genesee Hotel—
a place she never thought she'd be,
her face displaced by ecstasy,
and seemingly propelled
by the flapping of her skirt,
which reveals a stocking band

and a garter from a girdle.
She gives no signal
as to where or when she'll land.

She's horizontal. Like Superman.
Or a deep-sea diver on a reef,
with a knife between his teeth,
who knows where there are pearls.

DANCING ON THE EDGE

after Winslow Homer's A Summer Night

Who'd have guessed—
in such darkness—this moment of grace?—
where waves crash down from an inhuman space
and break into nothing, slip away
to nothing.

Among the grains that once were boulders,
the hermit crab finds the shell of
something long consumed.
It inserts its softer parts
and flails out its claw like the rest of us.

The trumpet worm busies itself with erecting its tube—
perfecting its illusion of salvation.
The kelp drops a thousand anchors
—not one of them will help—
time rolls in, does its work, rolls out—

and in the low tide in the morning:
the empty tube, the stranded length of kelp,
the shell where something's been consumed
—but tonight in the path of moonlight on the beach,
the domes of doomed
things gleam.

And even though you don't see any stars,
you'll make out the shapes along the shore:
the women, sitting on the sun-warmed rocks,
the men, standing, just a little way off,
and the children who don't answer
but keep leaping in the foam.

And you hear their voices say:
And did you enjoy the days
which are the only days,
and the nights
which are the only nights?

Sit down beside us now
where the ocean
sifts the boulders into sand,
where the headlong journey of a thousand miles
is stopped by a pile
of sand.

So you descend the shore till you're nearly at the edge—
but someone grabs your hand
and leads you up the slope
and holds you back
and looks into the dark for you
and takes your place.

And you keep pace with whoever it is—
as if this were life and death
with whoever it is—
who looks across your shoulder,
who lets you lean, who lets you rest—

who hums so close to your ear
that you don't hear the great-forever rush
of emptiness—
the crush and pull
of nothingness.

And yet it all seems so effortless—
even though it's more than a miracle—
that someone's swept you up
and holds you back from the leaden shapes
that wait on the shore like a ruin—

or that someone's turned your eyes
from the footprints you made just a moment ago—
already eroded,
washed out,
swallowed.

So you follow up the slope—
over the dried kelp,
over the shards of things that lost their hold—
because someone is holding you,
and your face, lit from within like a paper lantern,
holds firm against the gale,

and the waves stream behind you like banners,
and the red speck in the distance,
that keeps ringing out its warnings,
might not even
be there.

SONG OVERHEARD IN A FIELD

Softly, softly, the long grass sings:
"Someone's listening to our song—
let them have it tonight as they go off in the fog
to their warm white beds or the cold hard ground.
They will learn to sing our song
as the wheels come 'round.

"*There goes the couple* who were married in the morning
—in the chapel on the hill.
Now she waits in the dark like an untried lock
while he fumbles for the key.
He'll sing her our song as the tumblers turn.
By morning we'll count three.

"There goes the farmer to the barn with the lantern
—that lights his breath beneath the beams.
He leans his ear on his panting cow,
then rolls his weary sleeves.
He'll sing her our song as her calf spills down.
Tomorrow he'll find sleep.

"*There goes the mother* with her candle to the cradle
—to lift her baby to her breast.
Her rocker sails to summer
where his waves lap the shells on her chest.
She'll sing him our song as her lullaby.
And soon he'll be at rest.

"There goes the fiddler to the barn in the moonlight
—to stir the harvest with his strings.
Under the beams where the farmer's gone,
the dancers whirl like leaves.

They'll sing our song till the jigs are done.
Tomorrow they'll be sheaves.

"*There goes the widow* to her practice for the service
—in the chapel on the hill.
Her steps are slowed by the midnight frost
that slicks the mossy stones.
She'll sing our song as she plays her hymns.
By morning she'll come home."

Softly, softly, the long grass sings:
"The night is almost done. The wheels bring them 'round
on the old meridians to wait for another sun.
But the field keeps singing till the stars go out,
they've gone in the grass, and the wind's found a throat
—*and the clouds lie on the ground to listen.*"

Acknowledgments - continued from copyright page:

Poems from *Queen of the Mist* by Joan Murray, copyright © 1999 by Joan Murray. Used by permission of Beacon Press.

Poems from *The Same Water* by Joan Murray (published by Wesleyan University Press), copyright © 1990 by Joan Murray. Used by permission of the author.

NEW POEMS
The American Poetry Review for "The Gypsy Child" and "Rear View Mirror"
Cimarron Review for "The Ivory Billed One"
The Hudson Review for "Forsythia"
The Kenyon Review for "Funnel"
Luna for "The Copier" and "Lifeline"
Ontario Review for "Looking at the Birds," "Swimming for the Ark," "What Was Expected" and "Tomma and Sammy"
Ploughshares for "Family Dollar," "The Gardener's Wife," and "Max and Rose"
Poetry for "White Bridge Road"
Rattle for "The Witch's Daughter"
River Styx for "Just Taste Them" and "The Trees"
The Southern Review for "Wracked Blue Suitcase"
Southwest Review for "Deer in the Apples"

"Rear View Mirror" was selected for The Pushcart Prize.
"Deer in the Apples" was selected for Verse Daily.
"White Bridge Road" was selected for Poetry Foundation's Poem of the Day and syndicated to public radio stations via PRX's Poetry Off the Shelf.

The author wishes to acknowlede with gratitude:
The National Endowment for the Arts for the 2011 Poetry Fellowship which supported the writing of new poems in this collection, and Yaddo and The MacDowell Colony for the many residencies which supported the writing of new poems, as well as earlier ones.

JOAN MURRAY

Joan Murray is the author of prize-winning poetry books from W. W. Norton, Beacon Press and Wesleyan University Press. The winner of two National Endowment for the Arts' Poetry Fellowships, she was commissioned by Broadway's Jujamcyn Theaters to adapt her work for the stage. Her poems have appeared in many journals and anthologies, including *The Atlantic Monthly, Harper's, The Nation, The New York Times, The Best American Poetry* and *The Pushcart Prize,* and she has read her work on *Morning Edition, Bob Edwards Weekend, RadioLab* and other NPR shows. She has been Poet in Residence at the New York State Writers Institute, and is the editor of *The Pushcart Book of Poetry* and the *Poems to Live By* anthologies. A native of New York City, she lives with her husband in Old Chatham, NY.